AFTER IRAQ

ANARCHY AND RENEWAL IN THE MIDDLE EAST

GWYNNE DYER

Thomas Dunne Books
St. Martin's Press ❧ New York

For Ana Lucia and George

———•———

"Principle is OK up to a point,
but principle doesn't do any good if you lose."
– Dick Cheney, as White House Chief of Staff, 1976

THOMAS DUNNE BOOKS.
An imprint of St. Martin's Press.

www.thomasdunnebooks.com
www.stmartins.com

Library of Congress Cataloging-in-Publication Data

Dyer, Gwynne.
    [Mess they made]
    After Iraq: anarchy and renewal in the Middle East / Gwynne Dyer.—1st U.S. ed.
        p.   cm.
    ISBN-13: 978-0-312-37845-5
    ISBN-10: 0-312-37845-9
    1. Iraq War, 2003–   2. United States—Politics and government—2001–
3. Iraq—Politics and government—2003–   4. United States—Foreign relations—Middle East.   5. Middle East—Foreign relations—United States.   I. Title.

DS79.76.D94 2008
956.7044'31—dc22

                                                        2007046778

First published in Canada under the title *The Mess They Made: The Middle East After Iraq* by McClelland & Stewart Ltd.

First U.S. Edition: February 2008

10 9 8 7 6 5 4 3 2 1

CONTENTS

INTRODUCTION

The Middle East as we have known it for the past ninety years is coming to an end, because the Americans will soon be leaving. President Bush is so determined to resist that conclusion that the legions will not finally depart until he has left office, but it is coming as surely as the sun sets in the west. And although Bush will leave defeated and disgraced, he has set events and emotions in train that will transform the region – if not quite in the way he intended.

Ali Allawi, defence minister in the first American puppet government in Baghdad, got it exactly right in a regional peace proposal he floated recently: "The Iraqi state that was formed in the aftermath of the First World War has come to an end. Its successor state is struggling to be born in an environment of crises and chaos. The collapse of the entire order in the Middle East now threatens as the Iraq imbroglio unleashes forces in the area that have been gathering in virulence over the past decades."

Allawi is not exaggerating. The destruction of the Iraqi state and the subsequent defeat of U.S. military power there have finally destabilized the Middle East, a notional region that came into being after the collapse of the Ottoman empire in 1918 (though it did not become widely known as the "Middle East" until the Second World War). It was initially controlled by the British and French empires, who drew most of the borders, but a surge of revolutions in the 1940s and 1950s brought independence to the Arab countries. By then, however, both oil and Israel had made the region of great interest to the United States, which took over as the dominant power from the 1960s onwards. And under that American dispensation, there have been no further changes of regime for forty years, apart from the revolution in Iran in 1978 and the U.S. invasion of Iraq in 2003: the undemocratic regimes that were in power in 1967 are all still in power, within the borders that the European empires drew in 1918.

It is that Middle East that is now coming to an end. It is ending because defeat and humiliation in Iraq mean that soon there will no longer be the will in the United States to go on with the task of maintaining the status quo, and because the forces unleashed by the destruction of Iraq are going to overwhelm the status quo. Everything is now up for grabs: regimes, ethnic pecking orders within states, even the 1918 borders themselves might change. Five years from now there could be an Islamic Republic of Arabia, an independent Kurdistan, almost anything you care to imagine.

So what should the rest of the world do about this? Nothing. Just stand back and let it happen. Outsiders to the region have no solutions left to peddle any more (nor any credibility even if they did have solutions), and they no longer have the power or the will to impose their ideas. For the first time in a century, the region is going to choose its future for itself – and it may, of course, make a dreadful mess of it. Even then outsiders should not intervene, because foreign intervention generally makes things worse – but also because it's none of their business.

For several generations the West has insisted that the Middle East *is* its business, because that is where half the world's oil comes from. Radical change cannot be allowed there because it might interrupt the flow of oil, and so the region has remained politically and socially frozen for generations. But today every major oil-producing country in the Middle East depends on the cash flow from oil exports to feed its growing population, so they are all compelled to sell pretty much every barrel they can pump – and to sell it into a single global market that sets the price for buyer and seller alike. *So it doesn't matter to us who runs these countries.*

It matters a great deal to their own people, of course, but the oil will go on flowing no matter who's in charge, so it's all the same to the customers. If the new regime is better than the old, good; if not, too bad. But it's their business, not ours.

There is the question of Middle Eastern terrorism, but Islamist extremism and the terrorism it breeds are both responses to a century of foreign domination and manipulation of the region. It wouldn't all stop right away if the West ceased meddling in the area, but the resentment and humiliation that fuel it would dwindle rapidly. Just as well, because this is not a policy proposal; it is a prediction. The West *will* stop meddling in the region's affairs, because the United States is going home hurt.

Finally, the question of Israel. The Middle East was definitely the wrong place to put a Jewish state if the idea was to create a safe haven for the world's Jews, but that's done now and the question is: Will Israel survive? The answer is probably yes, because it has and will retain the ability to take the entire region down with it in a nuclear Armageddon. But the opportunity of the 1990s has been wasted, and it probably faces another generation of confrontation – perhaps, this time, without the comforting support of the United States.

What we are seeing at the moment is a clear demonstration, both to the American and the Middle Eastern publics, of the inability of American military power to dictate outcomes in the region. Once that demonstration has been concluded, we shall see what comes out of the box in the Middle East.

It will undoubtedly be messy, since it will be a sudden thaw after centuries of political glaciation under Ottoman rule, Anglo-French domination, and American hegemony. In places, it will probably be bloody. The West will not like some of the regimes that emerge (but it's *still* none of our business).

In the long run, it will certainly be better for the peoples of the region than perpetual foreign tutelage. And it will not harm the West's interests, so long as the oil continues to flow. Apart from that, the entire region is of little economic or strategic importance to the rest of the world. Lie back, and try to enjoy the ride.

CHAPTER I

THE HEART OF THE MESS

"We will soon launch an imperial war on Iraq with all the 'On to Berlin' bravado with which French poilus and British tommies marched in August 1914. But this invasion will not be the cakewalk neo-conservatives predict.

". . . Pax Americana will reach apogee. But then the tide recedes, for the one endeavour at which Islamic peoples excel is expelling imperial powers by terror and guerrilla war. They drove the Brits out of Palestine and Aden, the French out of Algeria, the Russians out of Afghanistan, the Americans out of Somalia and Beirut, the Israelis out of Lebanon. . . . We have started up the road to empire and over the next hill we will meet those who went before. "

– Pat Buchanan, *The American Conservative*, October 7, 2002

In early May 2003, a flight-suited President Bush flew out to the aircraft carrier *Abraham Lincoln* in order to have an appropriately military background, complete with "Mission Accomplished" banners, for his announcement of an end to "major combat operations" in Iraq. At that point, the Pentagon's expectation was that by the end of the year no more than thirty thousand U.S. troops would still be deployed in Iraq. Five years later, the number is still more than five times that many.

The resistance to the U.S. occupation really got underway a week before Bush's photo-op, in the dusty city of Fallujah, some fifty kilometres west of Baghdad. About a hundred U.S. troops from the 82nd Airborne Division had been deployed to Fallujah, and had taken up residence in the al-Kaat primary and secondary school, a pale yellow two-storey concrete building. Fallujah was a Sunni city where most people had backed the Ba'ath Party and some had benefited directly from its rule, and the American occupation was never going to be popular there. Rumours began to circulate, probably spread by former Baathist officials, that the Americans were peering into people's homes and ogling Muslim women with their night-vision goggles. Around nine o'clock on the evening of Monday, April 28, a crowd of between one hundred and two hundred young men marched to the school to demand that the Americans leave and the school be reopened.

What happened next will always be disputed. The commander of the American force, Lieut.-Colonel Eric Nantz, insists that his soldiers were shot at and that stones were thrown before they opened fire. However, the side of the building facing the street was completely unmarked by bulletholes, and witnesses unanimously said that they had seen no guns in the crowd. At any rate, thirteen young men were killed by the Americans, firing from the upper floor and the roof of the school, and many more were injured; no Americans were hurt. One Arab survivor of the confrontation, a nineteen-year-old student called Hassan who refused to give his last name, told British journalist Phil Reeves of the *Independent*: "We had one picture of Saddam, only one. There were quite a lot of us – about 200. We were not armed and nothing was thrown. There had been some shooting in the air, but that was a long way off. I don't know why the Americans started shooting. When they began to fire, we just ran." As Reeves was leaving the hospital the following day, he ran into the headmaster of the school, many of whose students had been among the victims, and the man calmly told him that he was willing to die as a "martyr" to take revenge against the Americans.

But it doesn't matter who was really responsible for the killing in Fallujah that night. If it hadn't happened there and then, something like it would have happened somewhere else in Iraq a little later.

"We didn't have enough troops on the ground. We didn't impose our will. And as a result, an insurgency got started and . . . it got out of control."
— Colin Powell, former U.S. secretary of state, former chairman, Joint Chiefs of Staff, April 2006

There has been endless debate in the United States about whether a different approach in the early days after the invasion could have avoided the rise of the insurgency. What if there had been twice as many troops in Iraq from the start? What if pro-consul Paul Bremer had not disbanded the Iraqi army and banned all Ba'ath Party members (including tens of thousands of school teachers, hospital doctors, and middle-rank civil servants who had been obliged to join the Party) from government employment? What if there had been an early transfer of power to an elected Iraqi government, as Jay Garner, the retired U.S. general originally chosen to run occupied Iraq, had been planning before he was abruptly replaced by Bremer? What if the occupation forces had managed to fix the electricity and water supply and protect the oil pipelines? But the might-have-beens are probably irrelevant. The U.S. invasion of Iraq was almost bound to produce a resistance movement.

"There were approximately ten demonstrators near a tank [outside an Iraqi military compound eight kilometres from Baghdad airport]. We heard a shot in the distance and we started shooting at them. They all died except for one. We left the bodies there. . . . The survivor was hiding behind a column about 150 metres away from us. I pointed at him and waved my weapon to tell him to get away. Half of his foot had been cut off. He went away dragging his foot. We were all laughing and cheering.

"Then an 18-wheeler [truck] came speeding around. We shot at it. One of the guys jumped out. He was on fire. The driver was dead. Then a Toyota Corolla came. We killed the driver, the other guy came out with his hands up. We shot him too.

"A gunny [gunnery sergeant] from Lima Company came running and said to us: 'Hey, you just shot that guy, but he had his hands up.' My unit, my commander and me were relieved of our command for the rest of the day. Not more than five minutes later, Lima Company took up our position and shot a car with one woman and two children. They all died. . . . In a month and a half, my platoon and I killed more than thirty civilians. . . .

"[Iraqis] would see us debase their dead all the time. We would be messing around with charred bodies, kicking them out of the vehicles and sticking cigarettes in their mouths. I also saw vehicles drive over them. It was our job to look into the pockets of dead Iraqis to gather intelligence. However, time and time again I saw Marines steal gold chains, watches and wallets full of money."

– Staff Sergeant (Ret'd) Jimmy Massey, USMC, about the
actions of the 7th Marines in early April 2003.
Quoted by Natashia Saulnier in "The Marine's Tale,"
The Independent, May 5, 2004

Any combat operation amidst a civilian population causes innocent casualties, and the U.S. military style, which is heavy on firepower and obsessed with "force protection" (shoot first and ask questions later), was bound to cause more civilian casualties than most. The fact that American troops were told that Iraqis were turning vehicles into suicide bombs (although there is only one documented case of that happening during the entire invasion) and dressing soldiers up as civilians made them doubly trigger-happy. They were young, they were frightened, and in most cases it was their first time in a really foreign country. They were bound to frighten and humiliate Iraqis, frequently out of sheer ignorance, and sometimes out of fear and hatred. On occasion, they were likely to panic and shoot indiscriminately – and it remains true that ordinary U.S. soldiers can shoot any Iraqi by whom they feel threatened without fear of the consequences. (Hundreds, perhaps thousands, of Iraqi farmers have been killed because they answered a knock on the door at night with a weapon in their hands in case of robbers, and were immediately shot by U.S. troops as suspected resistance fighters.) Iraqi culture is shaped by deeply held notions of honour and revenge, and individual Iraqis were bound to retaliate by attacking U.S. occupation troops. These factors alone would probably have produced a serious Iraqi resistance movement in time, but there was more.

First, there was the deep hostility to the United States felt by many people in every Arab country as a result of thirty-five years of reflex American support for Israel, and the additional hostility that accrued to the U.S. government in countries where it was seen as a supporter of the local dictator. Although nobody in Washington seems to have realized it, many Iraqis who hated Saddam Hussein, especially among the Shia majority, also saw him as an American puppet. He had co-operated with the CIA in exterminating the senior ranks of the Iraqi Communist Party (then largely Shia in membership) in the 1960s. Then, in 1980, he had attacked Shia Iran with U.S. support.

At the beginning of Saddam Hussein's invasion of Iran, all he had from Washington (so far as we know) was America's prayers that he could destroy the Islamic revolution in Iran. But by 1983, when Iraq was clearly losing the war, President Ronald Reagan sent a special envoy, Donald Rumsfeld, to

Baghdad to offer Saddam U.S. support in getting weapons, both conventional and unconventional. During the so-called "tanker war" in 1984–87, American warships protected oil-tanker convoys from Arab states from Iranian attacks, while Iraqi planes were left free to attack tankers sailing from Iranian ports. One Iraqi aircraft even struck a U.S. warship by mistake in 1986, killing thirty-seven American sailors, but as a de facto ally Baghdad was forgiven for its error. In 1988, an American warship accidentally shot down an Iranian airliner, killing 290 civilians, under the mistaken impression that it was an Iranian combat aircraft (it was in Iranian territorial waters at the time), but the American captain was forgiven, too.

Thanks to all the American help to Baghdad, the Iraq–Iran war ended in a draw in 1988, but Saddam Hussein abruptly terminated his de facto alliance with the United States, probably inadvertently, when he invaded Kuwait in August 1990. He should have known better, but there is evidence to suggest that he actually believed he had Washington's tacit assent to this invasion, and was taken aback when the United States reacted as it was bound to do. In the first Gulf War in 1991, the United States and a broad coalition of Western and Arab countries, operating under a UN mandate, liberated Kuwait and destroyed much of Saddam's army, but they did not overthrow him: the first President Bush, in office since 1989, obeyed his UN mandate and stopped short of driving north to Baghdad. What he did do, unfortunately, was urge the Shias of southern Iraq to rise in revolt at the end of the war – and then stand by while tens of thousands of them were massacred by Saddam's troops. So what many Iraqi Shias thought as they watched the 2003 war unfold was that America was sweeping its puppet aside at last and taking over Iraq directly. They were glad to see the end of

Saddam, but they didn't like or trust the replacement one bit.

The Sunni Arabs were an even trickier proposition, because the overthrow of the Ba'ath Party, their instrument of political domination, effectively meant the end of the centuries-long rule of the Sunni minority in Iraq. They were very unhappy about that, and they would be even more so when they discovered that they actually accounted for only about 20 per cent of Iraq's population (a fact not realized by most Sunnis in a country where statistics about the sectarian division were never published or openly discussed). To make matters immeasurably worse, in May 2003, the first head of the American-run Coalition Provisional Authority (CPA), retired American diplomat L. Paul Bremer III, disbanded the entire Iraqi army and police force and banned all senior Ba'ath Party members – and anybody in the top three management layers of government ministries, government-run corporations, universities, and hospitals who was a Party member at all – from future government employment. Bremer paid no heed to arguments that, until his arrival, conversations had been underway with Iraqi generals for the reconstitution of the army, purged of its Saddam loyalists, and that in all the former ruling parties of post-Communist states in the early 1990s the majority of the "senior" members had been innocent professionals who had been compelled to join in order to do their jobs.

So far as it can be discerned these were Bremer's own decisions, not imposed on him by the White House, and they had catastrophic effects. With a couple of decrees he effectively gutted the Iraqi state apparatus and abolished the only other national institutions, the army and police, that at least in theory rose above mere sectarian, ethnic, and local concerns. He also abruptly threw half a million people, most of them with weapons training, serious organizational abilities, or both, onto the street in the most humiliating way. The Sunni insurgency began at once, led initially by ex-army officers and Ba'ath officials and publicly justified by incidents like the killings at Fallujah. These "dead-enders," as they were explained away in Washington, were soon joined in the insurgency by homegrown Islamist extremists who had previously been terrorized into submission by Saddam's regime, and by some foreign Islamists, mostly from Saudi Arabia, who made themselves useful by offering to carry out suicide attacks. By the autumn of 2004, only a year and a half after the invasion, the U.S. authorities were recording between two thousand and three thousand insurgent attacks per month. The shocking pictures taken by the American torturers at Abu Ghraib had a big impact elsewhere in the Muslim world, but in Iraq they caused no particular upsurge in the violence: most people had already chosen their side.

Perhaps most damning of all, there was the astounding inability of the U.S. occupation forces to fix the infrastructures that had been broken in Iraq during the invasion and the subsequent orgy of looting, and the other things that had been broken long before that, so that Iraqis would at least experience some material improvement in their lives. Five months after the end of the first Gulf War in 1991, Saddam Hussein had managed to restore the supply of electricity in Iraq to the pre-war level despite the devastation and crushing sanctions; fifty months after the invasion of March 2003, the United States had failed to do as well: in late 2006, Baghdad was receiving an average of less than six hours' electricity a day. By any material measure, Iraqis today are worse off than they were under Saddam.

"Iraq was awash in cash – in dollar bills. Piles and piles of money. We played football with some of the bricks of $100 bills before delivery. It was a wild-west crazy atmosphere, the likes of which none of us had ever experienced."

– Frank Willis, former senior official,
Coalition Provisional Authority

"American law was suspended, Iraqi law was suspended, and Iraq basically became a free fraud zone. In a free fire zone you can shoot at anybody you want. In a free fraud zone you can steal anything you like. And that was what they did."

– Alan Grayson, Florida-based attorney prosecuting
CPA corruption, both men quoted in *Dispatches: Iraq's Missing Billions*, a Guardian Films production broadcast on
Britain's Channel Four on March 20, 2006

The first year was vital if popular satisfaction at the changes brought to Iraq by the invaders was to outweigh the many factors that were driving Iraqis towards resistance to the occupation, but in terms of reconstruction the first year was almost completely wasted. It wasn't for lack of money. Under Security Council Resolution 1483, passed on May 22, 2003, the United Nations, which had been enforcing sanctions against Iran, transferred some $23 billion of Iraqi money derived from frozen Iraqi bank accounts, seized Iraqi assets, and Iraqi oil sales into a Development Fund for Iraq and put it at the disposition of the American-run Coalition Provisional Authority in Baghdad. Shortly afterwards, the U.S. Congress voted a further $18.4 billion for the redevelopment of Iraq. That amounted to about $1,600 for every Iraqi man, woman, and child, which should have been enough to make a pretty big difference in the standard of everything from electricity supply to medical services in a low-wage economy like Iraq's. It made no difference at all.

In the first fourteen months, down to the "hand-over of sovereignty" and the end of the CPA ("children playing adults," as the U.S. military contemptuously called the young and inexperienced American staff, most of them chosen by patronage) in June 2004, only $300 million of the U.S. government's money was actually disbursed, but *all* of the Iraqi money was spent – although "spent" is perhaps the wrong word, as it implies an exchange of money for goods or services. Some $12 billion of the Iraqi money was flown from New York to Baghdad in cash – 363 tonnes of one-hundred-dollar bills – and handed out to Iraqi contractors (kickbacks galore), to American contractors with good connections in the Bush administration on inflated cost-plus contracts, and to "government ministries" in Baghdad that barely existed except on paper.

Some $800 million was handed over to U.S. military commanders for discretionary spending without being counted or even weighed. Another $1.4 billion was flown from Baghdad to the Kurdish regional government in Irbil, and has not been seen since. And the $8.8 billion that passed through the new government ministries in Baghdad during the reign of the CPA has never been accounted for, and there is little prospect of finding out where it went. The Defence Ministry's $1.3-billion procurement budget for 2005 vanished completely, together with the defence minister and the procurement chief: "It is possibly one of the biggest thefts in history," said Ali Allawi, finance minister at the time. The CPA itself kept one fund of nearly $600 million in cash for which there is simply no paperwork, and in the final month before it left Iraq, it managed to get rid of the last $5 billion of Iraq's money, most of it in contracts let without tender to American corporations with contacts in the White House. Auditors were not appointed until April 2004, and were not allowed to see the CPA's accounts, such as they were, until it had disbanded and gone home. It is likely that more money was stolen in the first year of the occupation of Iraq than Mobutu Sese Seko managed to steal in thirty-two years of looting the Congo.

Things improved slightly after that, because now it was American taxpayers' money being spent and Congress does insist on a certain level of accountability. But by the latter half of 2004, the insurgency was well underway in Iraq, and security was adding 25 per cent cost to almost every project undertaken in the country. Money also began to be diverted from the reconstruction fund to fight the insurgency, to build prisons, to prepare and conduct Saddam's expensive show trial, and to pay for two elections, a referendum, and four changes of government.

At least $2.5 billion originally meant for repairing infrastructure and schools was ultimately spent instead on building up Iraqi security forces, much of which would have been absorbed by the notorious "ghost battalions" whose commanders pocketed the pay of purely fictitious soldiers. Huge contracts continued to be let without tender to American companies to perform services that could have been provided far more cheaply by Iraqi contractors – and in early 2006 the Bush administration made it clear that when the $18.4 billion allocated by Congress for reconstruction ran out in June 2007, no further U.S. funds would be made available. In the end, probably less than $10 billion of the more than $40 billion that was made available for reconstruction immediately after the invasion was actually spent on reconstruction, and most of that was spent after the insurgents had begun to sabotage the infrastructure that the occupiers were trying to rebuild.

"I just presumed that what I considered to be the most competent national security team since Truman was indeed going to be competent. They turned out to be among the most incompetent teams in the postwar era. Not only did each of them, individually, have enormous flaws, but together they were deadly, dysfunctional."
— Kenneth Adelman, former special assistant to Donald Rumsfeld during his first term as secretary of defence (1975–77), in *Vanity Fair*, January 2007

Kenneth Adelman, former head of the Arms Control and Disarmament Agency under President Reagan, was a founding member of the Project for the New American Century (PNAC), a neo-conservative group in Washington that had urged the invasion of Iraq, and it was he who had promised that it would be a "cakewalk." It might therefore be thought somewhat ungracious of him to blame the ensuing disaster on the people who actually carried the invasion out – but then, the alternative would be to accept that he himself bore a large share of the blame for promoting the idea in the first place. Besides, even if the Iraq adventure were doomed to fail, Adelman was quite right about the quality of the leadership provided by the Bush administration. The occupation of Iraq was the most spectacularly incompetent and corrupt operation carried out by the government of any developed country in many decades, and it turned the high probability of a major insurgency in Iraq after the invasion into the certainty of countrywide violence, despair, and anarchy.

In early 2006, three years after the invasion, Iraq's national electricity grid was still only producing four thousand megawatts, 10 per cent below pre-war levels. Only a third of the population had access to clean water, most sewage was still going into the rivers untreated, and oil production was barely 2 million barrels a day, down from around 3 million barrels on the eve of the invasion. Unemployment in Iraq was variously estimated at between 40 and 70 per cent, and no construction cranes have been seen in Baghdad since the invasion with the exception of those strengthening the fortifications around "Coalition" bases and the Green Zone, the precinct in central Baghdad where the U.S. and British embassies and many U.S. military headquarters are now located. And as early as 2005, the sectarian killings were overtaking the deaths in the anti-American insurgency.

The principal instigator of the sectarian war was Abu Musab al-Zarqawi, the Jordanian-born Islamist whose provocatively named "Al-Qaeda in Mesopotamia" organization had been responsible for most of the truly horrendous terrorist attacks against innocent gatherings of Shia civilians during the preceding two years. He probably never had more than a few hundred followers – the Iraq Study Group chaired by former U.S. secretary of state James Baker and former chairman of the House Foreign Affairs Committee Lee Hamilton estimated at the end of 2006 that there were only thirteen hundred foreign fighters of all descriptions in Iraq – but Zarqawi's single-minded ruthlessness made him effective far beyond his numbers. As a Sunni extremist, he viewed Shias as heretics unworthy of the name of Muslim, and preventing Iraq from falling under Shia control was even more important to him than defeating the Americans (who would leave sooner or later in any case).

A stable, legitimate Iraqi government that was permanently dominated by a democratically elected Shia majority was the very last thing Zarqawi wanted to see, and so the Shias had to be lured into a civil war in order to destroy that possibility, however remote it might be. As late as 2004 there were still instances of co-operation between the mainstream Sunni resistance and Moqtada al-Sadr's (Shia) Mahdi Army, with the Sunnis supporting al-Sadr's uprising against the U.S. forces in Najaf that summer. The following autumn, some members of the Mahdi Army joined the defenders of Fallujah when that entirely Sunni city, having attacked American soldiers or mercenaries once too often, was effectively destroyed in a seven-week U.S. military operation, but that was the last instance of open Shia–Sunni military co-operation against the occupation forces: the steady stream of suicide-bomb atrocities against Shia civilians finally put an end to it. By mid-2005, Interior Ministry troops drawn from the (Shia) Badr Brigades were carrying out reprisal killings of Sunnis in very large numbers.

The two elections of January and December 2005, trumpeted in the Western media as triumphs of a nascent Iraqi democracy, had the practical effect of separating and alienating the various Iraqi communities even further. It is not clear whether the American authorities understood the implication of having everybody in the country vote for national "lists" of the competing parties, most of them defined by their ethnic or sectarian character, rather than choosing between different individual candidates in electoral districts as voters do in the United States, but the effect was to exclude all local needs and issues from the ballot. Instead, people ended up voting for the party that represented their ethnic or religious group, as that was in practice the only distinction among them, so all politics in Iraq became communal politics.

What is happening in Iraq is not a war between two communities of fanatics. Iraq has been one of the most secular countries in the Muslim world for a long time, and large numbers of those killed for being "Sunni" or "Shia" had not seen the inside of a mosque for years. Thousands of ordinary Iraqi citizens who wore their religion lightly or not at all have been stopped at a roadblock, pulled out of their cars, tortured and murdered just for having a "Shia" or "Sunni" name on their ID cards or a licence plate from the wrong province on their cars. It's a war about the numbers, the power and the will of rival communities that have been defined by their ancestral religious affiliations, not about what particular individuals believe today. It's a bit like the apocryphal story that did the rounds during the worst days of the sectarian war in Northern Ireland, where a motorist is stopped at a roadblock by armed, masked men who demand to know whether he is Catholic or Protestant. The wrong answer could get him killed, and he doesn't even know which side these gunmen are on, but the motorist thinks he has a perfect answer: "I'm a Jew." But it's not as easy as that. One of the gunmen snarls: "Are you a Catholic Jew or a Protestant Jew?"

The new police force on which the U.S. occupation authorities had placed such high hopes was a sectarian force from the start. After the bombing of the Askariya Mosque in Samarra, one of the holiest Shia shrines, on February 22, 2006, they and various Shia militia forces in Baghdad attacked at least two dozen Sunni mosques in the city with machine-gun fire and rocket-propelled grenades. From this point on, the ethnic cleansing of mixed neighbourhoods in the capital gained an unstoppable momentum.

"They say the killings and kidnappings are being carried out by men in police uniforms and with police vehicles, but everybody in Baghdad knows the killers and kidnappers are real policemen."
— Iraqi foreign minister Hoshyar Zebari, summer 2006. Quoted by Patrick Cockburn, *The Independent*, November 28, 2006

The man who had the biggest role in pushing Shia and Sunni Arabs into the endless tit-for-tat war of sectarian kidnaps, murders, and ethnic cleansing, Abu Musab al-Zarqawi, was killed in a U.S. air strike on June 7, 2006, but his legacy survives in the form of a mountain of mutilated corpses. By mid-2006, a hundred bodies a day were being found in Baghdad alone, and Manfred Nowak, the United Nations Special Rapporteur on Torture, reported that the bodies in the Baghdad morgue "often bear signs of severe torture including acid-induced injuries and burns caused by chemical substances, missing skin, broken bones (back, hands and legs), missing eyes, missing teeth, and wounds caused by power drills and nails." Those who were not killed by these tortures were finished off by a bullet to the head.

Even today, supporters of the invasion in the United States still warn that withdrawing U.S. troops would unleash civil war in Iraq, but that war actually began in 2006, and the clearest evidence for it is the scale of the refugee problem. The United Nations High Commissioner for Refugees (UNHCR) estimated in February 2007 that fifty thousand Iraqis a month were abandoning their homes, in order not to join the three thousand dead bodies that are found in sewers or on garbage heaps each month. That probably exceeds the monthly death toll in the early stages of either the English or the American civil wars, and it already matches the scale of killing at the peak of the war in Bosnia in the early 1990s. As in Bosnia, too, every major group, Sunni Arabs, Shia Arabs, and Kurds, sees itself as a victim, and all dealings among them are poisoned by "the politics of the last atrocity" (as they used to call it in Northern Ireland).

In most of Baghdad the ethnic cleansing has been so thorough that militants in adjacent Sunni and Shia neighbour-hoods now freely fire mortar rounds at each other, safe in the knowledge that they run little risk of hurting someone from their own group. At the beginning of 2007, the UNHCR estimated, there were about 1.8 million internal Iraqi refugees and another 2 million who had sought safety abroad, mostly in Syria or Jordan. ("Those with money go to Jordan. The poor go to Syria," observed John Pace, UN human rights chief in Iraq until early 2006.) The exiles include more than half the country's doctors and at least half of the smaller minority groups – Christians, Jews, Yazidi, Mandaeans, Palestinians, and Turkomans – who once accounted for a tenth of Iraq's population. It is likely that half of the educated and skilled middle class, which was the country's most valuable resource, has already left. If this does not count as a civil war, it will do until something worse comes along.

There remains a third internal war to be fought in Iraq, a Kurdish–Arab war that will erupt if the city of Kirkuk, its surrounding oil fields, and some other disputed territories in northern Iraq are not handed over to the autonomous government of Kurdistan after a referendum that is promised in the new constitution. However, that war may well be avoided, at least for a time, by a political deal between Kurdish and Shia Arab leaders, since the Kurds see some advantages in their current status. The Kurds are effectively independent, with their own Pesh Merga army thinly disguised as Iraqi army troops, yet they still enjoy great influence in Baghdad. They are also relatively safe from attack by their Turkish or Iranian neighbours, which are both determined to prevent the emergence of an independent Kurdish state, so long as they avoid a formal break with Iraq. But even if they manage to avoid this war – and also avoid a renewal of the chronic hostility between the two major Kurdish parties, the Kurdistan Democratic Party and the Patriotic Union of Kurdistan, which last flared into open war in the 1990s – the two wars that are already raging down south are enough to spell the end of the Iraqi state that was cobbled together in 1918–22 from the three former Ottoman *vilayets* (provinces) of Mosul, Baghdad, and Basra.

"The state is now moving inexorably under the control of the Shia Islamists, albeit with a supporting role for the Kurds. The boundaries of Shia-controlled Baghdad are moving ever westwards so that the capital itself may fall entirely under the sway of the Shia militias.

"The only thing stopping that is the deployment of American troops to block the entry of the Shia militias in force into these mixed or Sunni neighbourhoods. The geographic space outside Baghdad in which the insurgency can flourish will persist but the country will be inevitably divided. Under such circumstances, the power of the Shias' demographic advantage can only be counter-balanced by the Sunni Arabs' recourse to support from the neighbouring Arab states. It is inconceivable that such an outcome can possibly lead to a stable Iraqi state unless one side or another vanquishes its opponent or if the country is divided into separate states."

– Ali Allawi, Iraqi defence minister, trade minister, and finance minister, 2003–6, now senior adviser to Prime Minister Nouri al-Maliki, *The Independent*, January 5, 2007

"Ameriya, Jihad, Ghazaliyah, all these areas [of Sunni-controlled Baghdad] are becoming part of the new Islamic state of Iraq, each with an emir in charge. Each group is in charge of a specific street. We have defence lines, trenches and booby traps. When the Americans arrive we let them through, but if they show up with Iraqi troops, then it's a fight."
– Sunni insurgent commander Abu Aisha (a pseudonym),
speaking to Iraqi journalist Ghaith Abdul-Ahad,
The Guardian, January 13, 2007

The core political dilemma facing the U.S. occupation authorities in Iraq, from pro-consul Paul Bremer to former U.S. ambassador Zalmay Khalilzad, has been that they don't trust the Shias, but the Sunnis don't trust them. They wanted to create an Iraqi government that commanded popular support but gratefully acquiesced in America's desire for permanent military bases in the country ("enduring" bases, as they tactfully called them). That could only be a Shia-dominated government, since Shias account for about 60 per cent of the Iraqi population – but Washington didn't trust the major Shia parties in Iraq, because they were too close to Shia Iran. Indeed, most of their leaders had spent long years in exile in Iran during Saddam's rule. (This problem was one of the major considerations that had deterred George H.W. Bush's administration from marching on Baghdad in 1991.)

To the extent that the current Bush administration did any post-war planning, however, it presumed that after the "liberation" of Iraq in 2003 it would be able to construct a governing coalition in which Shia influence was heavily diluted by the presence of its Kurdish allies (the Kurds are the only group in Iraq that unequivocally supports the American presence) and of post-Baathist Sunni politicians who were willing to work with the United States. It also assumed that it had a lot of time to work on this project: ("We're going to be on the ground in Iraq, as soldiers and citizens, for years," said Bremer in March 2004. "We're going to be running a colony almost.") But it was wrong on both counts.

"The liberating force must act quickly because every army of liberation has a half-life after which it turns into an army of occupation," said General David Petraeus, one of the U.S. Army's leading counter-insurgency experts, but it was even worse than that. There was no time at all to act, because the Sunnis were instantly hostile to the American presence, while the Shias were determined from the start to parlay the weight of their numbers into irreversible domination of whatever new political system emerged in Iraq, and there really wasn't much Washington could do to satisfy either group.

What the Sunnis wanted back was the dominant position in Iraq that the American invasion had taken away from them, and there was no way the United States could deliver on that demand. All the Shias wanted was due democratic recognition of *their* newly acquired dominant role in Iraq, but Washington was extremely reluctant to deliver on that demand, either. It believed that the major Shia parties, the Supreme Council for Islamic Revolution in Iraq (SCIRI), which controls the powerful Badr Brigade, and al-Dawa (The Call), were both too close to Iran. (Indeed, the core units of the Badr militia had been trained by Iranians while they were in exile there.) And the third element in the Shia equation was a wild card called Moqtada al-Sadr, a radical young cleric (early thirties) who was strongly opposed to the American presence in Iraq. Al-Sadr, the surviving son of a revered ayatollah who had been murdered by Saddam, was very much the voice of the Shia poor, with his stronghold in the vast slum in northeastern Baghdad named after his martyred father, Sadr City – and his militia, the Mahdi Army, was the biggest in the country.

There was no combination of these forces that could possibly yield a democratically elected coalition government that wanted the United States to stay in Iraq, even assuming that it included the pro-American Kurds, so the U.S. dilemma was essentially insoluble from the start. Retired general Jay Garner was fired at the very beginning of the occupation for calling for early elections, and his replacement, Paul Bremer, adopted the short-term strategy of delaying elections indefinitely and relying on an appointed Iraqi government to put a local face on the occupation. Most of the people appointed were former exiles and all were pro-American, but by the time Bremer handed over "sovereignty" to that puppet government in June 2004, he had already been forced to abandon that strategy. In a confrontation with the senior Shia cleric in Iraq, the Iranian-born Grand Ayatollah Ali al-Sistani, in February and March 2004, Bremer had been forced to agree to genuine elections in 2005 in order to dissuade Sistani from calling a Shia general strike. After centuries at the bottom of the heap, the Shias were absolutely determined to assume the dominant role in the politics of a democratic Iraq that their numbers entitled them to. They were willing to do it legally through the ballot box, but they were not willing to wait.

The two elections and the constitutional referendum of 2005 did give Iraq the legal structure of a constitutional, parliamentary democracy – and a National Assembly whose members have been elected to govern the country until 2009. It is even possible that this structure will survive the departure of the Americans, and that whatever kind of Iraq emerges in the aftermath will continue to be governed by more or less democratic means. But most Sunni Arabs boycotted the elections and consequently are not properly represented in the National Assembly and the government, thus deepening their alienation from the emerging new order in Iraq, and the mutual hostility of the various ethnic and sectarian factions that are present makes it difficult to create a government that works. It took 67 days of negotiations to form a government after the January 2005 elections, and 127 days after those of December 2005.

"The ministries are beyond repair. Officials were corrupt under Saddam Hussein but frightened to death of being executed. Not any more."
– Zuhair Hamadi, chief of staff to the cabinet in the government of Iyad Allawi, 2004–5. Quoted by Patrick Cockburn, *The Independent*, October 14, 2005

In practice, each group that is included in the government is granted one or more ministries that it then runs as a private fiefdom and cash machine. Ministers cannot be replaced, no matter how corrupt or incompetent, without reopening the lengthy, Byzantine negotiating process that created the government in the first place. In the case of the Interior Ministry, which was run by a minister from the SCIRI party until well into 2006, the party's militia, the Badr Brigade, simply moved inside the ministry and re-emerged as a dominant presence in the police force. (The Interior Ministry has been run by a less partisan figure, at American insistence, since the installation of Nouri al-Maliki's government in April 2006, but the Badr Brigade still has a stranglehold on the middle and senior ranks of the Interior Ministry police.) The complete collapse of security in Baghdad has also made the top level of government very remote from the country it allegedly rules, with most ministers taking shelter in the Green Zone. Some visit their ministries frequently, others less often or (rumour has it) not at all, instead having papers brought to the Green Zone for signature. It would be a most unsatisfactory system, with no coordination of government policy and no cabinet responsibility, even if it were not subject to constant manipulation by the occupying power.

U.S. policy in dealing with the cumbersome and deeply flawed but undeniably Iraqi beast it has created has had three general priorities. One is to push continually for greater participation by Sunni Arabs, even if holding another election to increase their formal representation before 2009 is out of the question. The anti-occupation insurgency backed by that group was until recently the greatest challenge faced by the U.S. authorities, and they have searched diligently (if unsuccessfully) for ways to reconcile them to the new order. They also want them to be more present in politics, to dilute the Shia domination of the whole process.

The second priority has been to keep Iranian influence at a minimum, which has required frequent interventions in the negotiations among the Shia parties in order to ensure that the "wrong" candidates are not selected for senior government posts. One of the main reasons for the lengthy delay in choosing a prime minister after the election of December 2005, for example, was the fact that the United States believed that Ibrahim al-Jaafari, the first choice of the Shia parties, was too close to Iran and to Moqtada al-Sadr, a particular *bête noire* of Washington's because he keeps demanding that the United States leave Iraq. In the end, the Shias gave in and chose Nouri

al-Maliki, a leader of the Dawa party, for the prime ministership instead.

The third American priority has been to ensure that there is
no public demand for a timetable for the withdrawal of foreign
troops. This paralyzes the government's attempts to seek reconciliation with the Sunni Arabs and to deal with the problem
of the sectarian militias, since a prerequisite is just such a
timetable. Not long after he became prime minister in April
2006, Nouri al-Maliki came up with a twenty-eight-point
national reconciliation proposal modelled on the post-
apartheid program in South Africa: militants would be par-
doned, those in jail would be freed, arms would be handed in,
and everybody would have a fresh start. All the major groups
expressed interest, but it was vetoed by the United States
because the deal necessarily and inevitably included the
promise of a timetable for American withdrawal from Iraq.
The proposal might well have fallen at the next hurdle anyway,
for Iraq was pretty far gone by 2006, but it might also have
been the last chance for a settlement that keeps everybody in
the same country.

We will never know if it was or not, but this is a good point
at which to ask the question: *Why* does the United States government not want to accept a timetable for the withdrawal of
American troops from Iraq? If the Bush administration were
really looking for a good excuse to wash its hands of the mess,
what could be more welcome than an official request from the
elected government of Iraq to send the troops home? It could
be presented to the American public as a triumph of democracy, and most of the Iraqis now trying to kill American soldiers would be glad to stop fighting and let them leave in
peace, and even with some face saved, so long as it was certain

that they were all really leaving. What would happen after-wards in Iraq is impossible to say, but it *might* be possible to preserve a democratic system and restore government author-ity over most of the country even at this late date. If not, the United States would be free to tell itself that it did all it could, but you just cannot teach those Ay-rabs civilized ways. Blaming the victim is always popular.

Instead, the U.S. authorities in Iraq expend a great deal of energy in ensuring that an official request for the withdrawal of foreign troops does not see the light of day. The only logical explanation is that, while the Bush administration would love to bring most of the troops home and ease the political pres-sure there, it still has not accepted the necessity of bringing them *all* home. It still imagines, in some incoherent way, that it can manipulate events in Iraq so that the insurgency dies down, the economy stabilizes, and a grateful Iraqi government welcomes the permanent stationing of twenty or thirty thou-sand American troops on its territory. The fourteen "enduring bases," with which the White House planned to replace the bases in Saudi Arabia that had become a political liability for the Saudi government, are still under construction, and as far as the White House and the Pentagon are concerned the game is still afoot. Chickens do tend to run around for a bit even after their heads are chopped off.

The contempt that both Iraqis and other Arabs feel for the Iraqi government is in large measure a by-product of this American policy, because in order to avoid demands for with-drawal the Iraqi government must be kept weak. Prime Minister al-Maliki has publicly said that he cannot move even a company of soldiers without U.S. permission. It is the CIA that pays the entire budget of the main Iraqi intelligence service, not the Iraqi government, so guess who it works for. And although the financial arrangements in Iraq remain as obscure as ever, it is clear that al-Maliki's government, unable to raise anything like the amount of revenue it needs from the devastated Iraqi economy, is on a very short financial leash held by the Americans. Any other Iraqi government operating under the ultimate control of the U.S. occupation forces will suffer a similar lack of credibility, so the long-term shape of post-Saddam Iraq will not even start to become clear until there is a complete American troop withdrawal, or at least a high-speed timetable for a withdrawal with hard dates attached. How might Iraq get from here to there, and what will that final shape be?

"The implosion of domestic support for the war will compel the disengagement of U.S. forces; it is now just a matter of time. Better to withdraw as a coherent and at least somewhat volitional act than to withdraw later in a hectic response to public opposition . . . or a series of unexpectedly sharp reverses on the ground. . . . If it gets really tough in the next few months, it will throw fuel on the fire in Washington. Congress will be emboldened in direct proportion to the trouble in Iraq."
– Steven Simon, former director for transnational threats on the National Security Council during the Clinton administration, in a paper for the Council on Foreign Relations, February 2007

There is no doubt about the implosion of domestic support in the United States for the Iraq war. By mid-2006, despite years of deliberate obfuscation by the administration, a *New York Times/CBS News* poll revealed that a majority of Americans had finally grasped that the war in Iraq was quite separate from the "war on terror." The Republicans' loss of control in both houses of Congress to the Democrats in the November 2006 mid-term elections was widely interpreted as a national vote against the war. By early 2007, when President Bush announced that he was planning to send more than twenty thousand extra U.S. troops to Iraq (a number subsequently increased to almost forty thousand), a *Washington Post*/ABC poll showed that 61 per cent of Americans opposed the plan while only 36 per cent backed it. Public opinion fluctuates over time on most issues, but it is hard to imagine what events in Iraq could reverse the long-term decline in American support for the war before the 2008 election.

There is a good deal more doubt, however, about the willingness of Congress simply to cut off supplies for the war. Bush will probably be able to go on trying to reverse the verdict on a war that most other people (including most soldiers) believe is already lost right down to the end of his term, for with so little time left before the presidential election in November 2008, the Democrats in Congress will be tempted to leave him twisting in the wind rather than accept the political burden of having "betrayed" American troops on the battlefield. But the speed with which American public opinion is now moving against the war suggests that no presidential candidate of either party who does not promise withdrawal from Iraq will stand much chance of winning the 2008 election, so the likeliest time for the announcement of a comprehensive American troop withdrawal from Iraq is about ten minutes after the inauguration of the 44th U.S. president, whether he or she is Democratic or Republican, in January 2009.

We can see that far ahead with some confidence, but what happens next? Will the heavens fall in the Middle East, and if so, on whose head? Does the U.S. military just retreat to

Kuwait, Bahrain, and other nearby countries to await events, or will this be the start of an American pullout from the entire region? Where, exactly, does the Middle East fit into U.S. grand strategy, assuming that there is such a thing?

Everybody knows that American strategy in the Middle East is "about oil," but what, exactly, does that mean? Maybe that is the best place to start.

CHAPTER II

WHY IRAQ?

"I now regret that I did not more openly challenge those who were determined to invade a country whose actions were peripheral to the real threat – al-Qaeda."

– Lieut.-General Gregory Newbold, USMC (ret'd), April 9, 2006.
Newbold, the former director of operations at the
Joint Staff (Pentagon), was the only senior military officer
to resign over the plan to invade Iraq.

I t's the great puzzle of the early twenty-first century: Why did the United States choose to invade Iraq? There was never a shred of plausible evidence to suggest that the Iraqi regime was in contact with the al-Qaeda terrorists, nor indeed would that have made any sense in terms of Saddam Hussein's politics and beliefs: his regime's principal contact with local Iraqi Islamists was in the torture chamber.

Saddam was certainly a loose cannon, as his foolish invasion of Kuwait in 1990 had amply demonstrated, and the ensuing Gulf War spelled the end of the loose U.S.–Iraqi alliance that had been forged after Saddam's invasion of Iran in the 1980s. But the Iraqi armed forces were comprehensively trashed during Operation Desert Storm in 1991, and the subsequent arms embargo had made it virtually impossible for them to rebuild: in the twenty-first century, Iraq posed no real military threat to any of its neighbours. And, of course, it had no "weapons of mass destruction," although perhaps we should be charitable and concede that the Bush administration may have come to believe its own propaganda on that question in the end.

Even so, nobody in the administration or in the "intelligence community" in Washington believed that Iraq had *nuclear* weapons. (If they had, then Iraq would never have been invaded, for the same obvious reason that North Korea was not invaded.) The only WMD that anyone thought Saddam might possess were chemical and biological weapons – and frankly, *everybody* in the Middle East has those. Iraq had certainly had them in the 1980s, and had used poison gas extensively in its war against Iran in 1980–88. The Reagan administration in the United States, Saddam's de facto ally at the time, protected him from international diplomatic condemnation over his persistent use of chemical weapons against Iranian troops, and turned a blind eye to his purchase of the chemical precursors for mustard gas and sarin and VX (nerve gas) and equipment for manufacturing them from various U.S. allies (Germany, the Netherlands, Italy, Egypt, and Singapore were the most important suppliers). The CIA even provided Iraq with "data from sensitive U.S. satellite reconnaissance photography . . . to assist Iraqi bombing raids," according to a *Washington Post* report of December 15, 1986, although Washington was well aware that those bombing raids frequently included chemical attacks – and more than sixty officers of the Defense Intelligence Agency worked to provide Baghdad with "detailed information on Iranian deployments, tactical planning for battles, plans for air strikes and bomb-damage assessments for Iraq," according to a *New York Times* report of August 17, 2002.

But Iran has chemical weapons, too, and so does Syria, not to mention U.S. allies like Israel and Egypt (which used poison gas during its intervention in one of Yemen's civil wars in the 1960s). Even if Washington were genuinely concerned about some Middle Eastern country giving chemical weapons to terrorists, there was no particular reason to worry more about Iraq than Iran or Syria.

Logic has its limits, so we must always remain open to the possibility that the key decision-makers in the Bush administration were so ill-informed that they simply did not understand these basic facts about the Middle East. It is possible that Bush himself cannot tell, or cannot be bothered to tell, the difference between one bunch of Arabs and another, so that the linkage he constantly makes between the al-Qaeda terrorists who attacked the United States and the Baathist regime in Iraq, which had nothing whatever to do with them, sounds perfectly reasonable to him. But surely those around him must have known better, comes the automatic protest – but it's clear that not all of them did. Consider the curious case of Dr. Henry Kissinger.

Kissinger, who served as Richard Nixon's secretary of state and national security adviser during the Vietnam War, has become a close adviser to President Bush as the situation in Iraq comes to resemble the quagmire that Kissinger faced in Vietnam thirty-odd years ago, and we now know, thanks to Robert Woodward's third book on the Bush presidency, *State of Denial*, that Kissinger can't be bothered to make distinctions among Arabs either.

"Why did you support the Iraq War?" [senior White House speech-writer Michael Gerson asked Kissinger in September 2005].

"Because Afghanistan wasn't enough," Kissinger answered. In the conflict with radical Islam, he said, they want to humiliate us. "And we need to humiliate them." The American response to 9/11 had essentially to be more than proportionate – on a larger scale than simply invading Afghanistan and overthrowing the Taliban.

Something else was needed. The Iraq War was essential to send a larger message, "in order to make a point that we're not going to live in this world that they want for us."

The deaths of four thousand American soldiers and several hundred thousand Iraqis would not seem an unreasonable price to pay for making that point to the man who unleashed even worse mayhem on Cambodia in order to make a point to Vietnam, but who is this "they" that he wants to make the point to this time? Radical Islam, presumably. How does he accomplish that by overthrowing the regime of Saddam Hussein, the head of a secular Arab regime and one of the most relentless enemies of radical Islam? Could Kissinger have been so ignorant that he simply did not know which side Saddam was on? Surely not, for he has a Ph.D., a German accent, and thick glasses. Was he so intellectually lazy that he just didn't care? Perhaps.

While Bush insisted that invading Iraq was about terrorism and WMD, most of his opponents insisted that it was about oil, but that doesn't make much sense either, at least in the conventional sense that the United States was seeking to "secure its oil supplies" or to bring down the oil price. There is no need to "secure" the oil supply when the supplier is more than willing to sell it to you (Iraq sold half its oil exports to the United States even in the last month before the invasion), and the price issue was already taken care of: America's Saudi Arabian ally has done sterling work over the years in adjusting its huge oil production upwards or downwards so as to keep world oil prices within a comfortable band most of the time. Yet there was the ghost of a strategy here, for Middle Eastern oil had once been a strategically sensitive commodity.

The original U.S. diplomatic and military commitments in the Middle East were made during the Cold War, when access to oil supplies, as to other strategic resources, was a zero-sum game in which a gain by one side was automatically a loss for the other. The strategists on either side calculated that if the Soviet Union or the United States had the predominant influence over a given regime, then in a crisis its oil, uranium, or whatever would not be available to the other side. This never made as much sense as the prevailing strategic doctrine pretended, since crises during the Cold War tended to be brief – either you backed away from the confrontation, or you accepted the likelihood of a nuclear war – but it provided the rationale for a generation's worth of American and Soviet meddling in the internal affairs of the Arab countries and Iran. It was also the context in which the United States first forged its close military alliance with Israel, which successfully convinced Washington that it was the indispensable cornerstone of the American strategic presence in the region.

All that is ancient history now. The Cold War ended almost twenty years ago, and since then it really hasn't mattered from a strategic point of view whether Country A is "pro-American" or "pro-Russian." There isn't going to be a military confrontation between the United States and Russia, and Country A will gladly sell its oil to the highest bidder regardless of ideology or alliances. By the same token, the U.S.–Israeli alliance no longer serves Washington's strategic purposes, especially since it comes with such a high diplomatic cost.

The strategic logic said that the zero-sum game was over and that the United States should cut back sharply on its military and diplomatic investment in the Middle East, leaving the Arab countries to run their domestic affairs as they chose and withdrawing the unconditional U.S. military guarantee of Israel's security. Had Washington acted on this logic, some Arab regimes would probably have been overthrown sooner or later by their long-suffering people, the United States would have saved a great deal of money, and Israel would have been forced to make some hard choices between its desire for more territory and its need for a secure peace with its Arab neighbours, including the Palestinians. But the strategic logic was ignored, and the U.S. military presence in the region did not diminish. On the contrary, it grew.

There was a variety of reasons for this, though no good ones. Commercial interests, particularly in the oil industry, successfully lobbied the U.S. government for support in their dealings with various oil-rich Arab states, and that support generally entailed arms sales and political backing for the regime in question. The official U.S. obsession with Iran, almost as irrational as the comparable obsession with Cuba and by now more than half as old, made it very hard for American policy-makers simply to leave the regime in Tehran alone. Israel fought a persistent and largely successful public relations battle to persuade the U.S. Congress and the American public that the American–Israel alliance continued to serve the strategic interests of the United States as well as those of Israel. Above all, the U.S. military-industrial complex (as President Dwight D. Eisenhower baptized it in his farewell address in 1961) did precisely what you would expect an interest group of that nature to do: it worked to preserve and if possible expand American military commitments abroad and the list of "threats" to U.S. interests, in order to create more work for its members.

So for almost two decades now, the military and political power of the United States in the Middle East has been dedicated to the task of preserving the status quo, even though the post–Cold War strategic logic said that its commitments there should be shrinking. Arab regimes that have long passed their "best before" date, like those of Hosni Mubarak in Egypt and the National Liberation Front generals in Algeria, have been tacitly supported by the United States in the repression of their own people. Israel has been licensed to use grossly disproportionate force against both Lebanon and the Palestinians, and to demand substantial chunks of the remaining Palestinian territories as its price for letting the Palestinians have a state. Iran has been demonized, isolated, and subjected to an American trade embargo enforced with the same manic enthusiasm as the one against Cuba. None of this served American interests, and the result was entirely predictable, although apparently not predicted by U.S. policy-makers: radicalization right across the region.

Even in the best of all worlds there would have been a degree of radicalization in the politics of the Arab Middle East in the past couple of decades. The regimes that emerged as the major players in the post-colonial Arab world in the 1950s and 1960s, whether they were monarchies that had achieved a certain national legitimacy like those of Saudi Arabia and Jordan or republics ruled by soldiers professing a faith in "Arab socialism" like Egypt, Iraq, and Syria, had all conspicuously failed to deal with the problems created by the birth of Israel. Those not endowed with large quantities of oil had also failed to provide a decent living standard for their people. By the 1980s and 1990s, there was a widespread feeling in the Arab world that the regimes' time was up, and that it was time to try something different.

The new revolutionary movements were predominantly Islamist in ideology, and some of them were very radical indeed. But this would have remained a matter of concern only to the Arabs themselves if the United States had begun cutting its military commitments in the region as the strategic importance of the area dwindled following the Cold War. Instead, by nominating itself as the key supporter of the status quo throughout the Arab world, the U.S. government eventually turned Americans into targets for Islamist attacks.

The first Bush administration (1989–92), the Clinton administration (1993–2000), and the current Bush administration all contributed to this policy disaster, but in defence of the first President Bush it can be pointed out that he faced a special problem: it was on his watch that Saddam Hussein invaded Kuwait. It was an act of wanton international aggression of precisely the kind that the United Nations had been created to prevent, and in the early post–Cold War years President George H.W. Bush, a man of immense international experience, was trying to restore the credibility of the UN rules, so he seized on the Iraqi invasion of Kuwait as an opportunity to demonstrate that those rules, if properly applied, really could make the world a safer place. He also had the legitimate concern that Saddam Hussein, having gained control of Kuwait's enormous oil reserves, might next target Saudi Arabia's adjacent Eastern Province, the largest oil reservoir in the world.

The coalition that the elder Bush put together in 1990 to oust America's erstwhile ally from occupied Kuwait was constructed in strict obedience to UN rules and with explicit Security Council approval. It included military contributions from most of the major Arab states (including Syria, whose regime was normally hostile to the United States), and it restricted itself to the sole task of liberating Kuwait. It was a rare moment of relative clarity in American policy towards the Middle East, and Bush Sr. followed up the easy military victory that liberated Kuwait by compelling Israel to attend the international conference in Madrid that he summoned after the war to discuss a general peace settlement in the region. But months later he was gone, defeated by Clinton in the 1992 election.

Bill Clinton made a brief attempt to broker an Israeli–Palestinian peace settlement late in his second term (2000), but generally adhered to the default American foreign policy setting of support for the status quo in the Middle East. He seems never to have questioned how deeply the United States should be committed militarily in the region, and shared the growing obsession in Washington with the "unfinished business" of Saddam's regime in Iraq, which he bombed heavily on several occasions. American policy towards the Middle East stayed on autopilot, with few exceptions, until President George W. Bush took office in January 2001. But then it changed radically – *before* 9/11. The Bush administration wanted to invade Iraq from the moment it took office, but not because of terrorism, or WMD, or the alleged search for secure oil supplies.

Even now, it is hard to exaggerate just how radical George W. Bush's defence and foreign policy team was in the early days, compared to the random collection of policy wonks and elected politicians with an amateur interest in foreign affairs who ran the show in earlier administrations. Nothing like it had been seen in Washington since the high-powered team of "defence intellectuals" whom John F. Kennedy installed in the White House, the Pentagon, and the State Department in 1961, and the result was eerily similar. The younger President Bush's team arrived in office with a coherent analysis of the geo-political situation of the United States and a grand strategy for maintaining America's dominant role in the world that would have impressed Admiral Alfred T. Mahan or Sir Halford

Mackinder, grand geopolitical theorists of a century ago. They were, in other words, very dangerous people.

The professional and ideological roots of the "neo-conservatives" and their hardline nationalist allies in the first Bush administration are common knowledge by now, but a few key points are still not widely understood. Primary among them is the shift in this group's perspective from the elation and blind triumphalism of the early 1990s, when all things seemed not only possible but easy, to the much more measured strategic calculations they were making by the late 1990s, by which time it was clear that history had not ended.

The hyperventilation of the early post–Cold War era was most vividly displayed in the Defense Planning Guidance (DPG) that was produced by Paul Wolfowitz and Lewis "Scooter" Libby under the direction of Secretary of Defense Richard Cheney only months after the final collapse of the Soviet Union in December 1991. As Democratic Senator Robert C. Byrd described it to the *Washington Post* on March 11, 1992, "The basic thrust of the document seems to be this: We love being the sole remaining superpower in the world and we want so much to remain that way that we are willing to put at risk the basic health of our economy and well-being of our people to do so."

"Our first objective is to prevent the re-emergence of a new rival.

"This is a dominant consideration . . . and requires that we endeavor to prevent any hostile power from dominating a region whose resources would, under consolidated control, be sufficient to generate global power. These regions include Western Europe, East Asia, the territory of the former Soviet Union, and Southwest Asia.

"There are three additional aspects to this objective: First, the U.S. must . . . (convince) potential competitors that they need not aspire to a greater role or pursue a more aggressive posture to protect their legitimate interests. Second, in the non-defense areas, we must account sufficiently for the interests of the advanced industrial nations to discourage them from challenging our leadership or seeking to overturn the established political and economic order. Finally, we must maintain the mechanisms for deterring potential competitors from even aspiring to a larger regional or global role."
— Draft Defense Planning Guidance, February 1992

There was a striking lack of ideology in the draft Defense Planning Guidance, a document intended to provide a planning context for U.S. defence officials for the rest of the decade, because the cherished Republican myth about how the power of American ideals, as expressed by Ronald Reagan, had brought down the "evil empire" was not yet a major part of American political discourse. The ambition, however, was breathtaking: the DPG examined the possibility of maintaining America's newly acquired position of sole superpower over the long term, and concluded that it could be done.

All that would be required was somewhat bigger defence budgets than those of the Cold War, so that the United States could maintain permanent military pre-eminence over all of Europe and Asia. That would enable it to deter potential rivals, including current allies like Germany and Japan, "from even aspiring to a larger regional or global role." Countries suspected of trying to develop weapons of mass destruction should face pre-emptive attack. U.S. military interventions overseas would, in this (allegedly desirable) future, be a "constant feature," and might well include the pre-emptive use of American nuclear, biological, and chemical weapons.

If you omit the technological and political references specific to our own time, you can easily imagine such a document being produced by the strategic advisers to Charles v in 1520, after his election as Holy Roman Emperor added most of Germany to his Spanish possessions: you are now the dominant power in the world, Your Majesty; here's how to stay in the saddle. It's even easier to imagine a comparable document being produced in Britain after victory at Waterloo in 1815 set the British empire up as the nineteenth century's sole superpower, if only Defense Planning Guidances had been in fashion at the time. But it was truly a bizarre document for late twentieth-century Washington.

To begin with, the people of the American republic do not like foreign wars. They have been encouraged, over the past thirty or forty years, to glory in the sheer scale and destructive power of U.S. military forces, but wars waged merely to safeguard the global strategic position and the "prestige" of the United States are alien to the deepest traditions of the republic. Such conflicts also kill the children of American voters in places whose names they do not even recognize. Foreign wars of more than one or two months' duration almost invariably end up as a political liability in late twentieth- and early twenty-first-century America.

Secondly, the world has changed. The traditional great-power game of seventeenth- and eighteenth-century Europe, with a pecking order determined by the size of population and economic resources and reordered by the occasional decisive military victory, has long since given way to subtler calculations of technological prowess, financial leverage, and cultural

influence, and there are hardly ever "decisive military victories." The authors of the 1992 Defense Planning Guidance were
people with an archaic worldview that had little currency
outside military/strategic circles, and they were promptly
brought to heel by more sophisticated people who did understand how the world now works.

The designated grown-up who intervened in 1992 to deal
with this embarrassing document was James Baker, the senior
President Bush's secretary of state, who made the boys clean it
up and tone it down. Like "41" (the family nickname for the
forty-first president of the United States – Bush Sr.), Baker saw
the world as a web of institutions and rules and relationships,
not just a theatre for the exercise of raw military power (and he
probably didn't believe in the miraculous healing power of
American democracy, either). But the views of both the hardline nationalists and their neo-conservative allies did evolve
between 1992, the last year of the long Republican ascendancy
in Washington, and 2000, the eve of their return to power.

Much has been written about the group of senior
Republicans, mostly people who had held defence and foreign
policy jobs during the presidencies of Ronald Reagan and
George H.W. Bush, who came together in 1997 as the Project for
the New American Century (PNAC), an ad hoc pressure group
sharing the offices of the American Enterprise Institute (AEI) in
Washington. Their first major public initiative was an open
letter to President Bill Clinton in January 1998 demanding that
he invade Iraq, but it had nothing in particular to do with U.S.
strategy in the Middle East, let alone with any alleged terrorist
threat from there. Even three years later, when most of the signatories of that letter had been appointed to leading positions
in George W. Bush's first administration – Donald Rumsfeld

(secretary of defence), Paul Wolfowitz (deputy secretary of defence), Peter Rodman (assistant secretary of defence for international security affairs), Richard L. Armitage (deputy secretary of state), Paula Dobriansky (undersecretary of state for global affairs), John Bolton (undersecretary of state for arms control and international security, U.S. ambassador to the UN), Elliott Abrams (special assistant to the president, senior director on the National Security Council for Near East and North African affairs), Zalmay Khalilzad (ambassador to Afghanistan, ambassador to Iraq, ambassador to the UN), Robert B. Zoellick (U.S. trade representative, deputy secretary of state), and Richard Perle (member of the Defense Policy Board) – they showed little interest in terrorist threats. The White House counter-terrorism chief in the first months of the Bush administration, Richard A. Clarke, is bitterly eloquent in his 2004 book, *Against All Enemies*, about the near-impossibility of getting these people to pay attention to the growing threat of an al-Qaeda attack on the United States during the seven months between President Bush's inauguration and the 9/11 attacks. Yet they wanted to invade Iraq.

Clarke goes ballistic when he describes the scene in the White House the morning after 9/11. "I expected to go back to a round of meetings examining what the next attacks could be, what our vulnerabilities were, what we could do about them in the short term. Instead I walked into a series of discussions about Iraq. At first I was incredulous that we were talking about something other than getting al Qaeda. Then I realised with almost a sharp physical pain that Rumsfeld and Wolfowitz were going to try to take advantage of this national tragedy to promote their agenda about Iraq. Since the beginning of the administration, indeed well before, they had been pressing for a war with Iraq. My friends in the Pentagon had been telling me that the word was we would be invading Iraq sometime in 2002."

His friends in the Pentagon turned out to be wrong by a year, because the 9/11 attacks meant that President Bush first had to deal with Afghanistan (where the al-Qaeda terrorists were actually based) before he could go on to invade Iraq. But the terrorist attacks of 9/11 did give the Bush administration what it had previously lacked: a pretext for invading Iraq plausible enough for public consumption. All it had to do was to manufacture some fake evidence linking Saddam Hussein with al-Qaeda (that was Doug Feith's job at the Pentagon's newly created Office of Special Plans) and rely on the laziness and cowardice of the mass media and the ignorance and knee-jerk nationalism of the general public to do the rest.

But none of the pre-9/11, uncooked intelligence had ever linked Iraq and al-Qaeda, and yet Iraq had been at the top of their hit list for years. As former treasury secretary Paul O'Neill recalled in Ron Suskind's 2004 book, *The Price of Loyalty: George W. Bush, the White House, and the Education of Paul O'Neill*, he saw a secret dossier titled "Plan for Post-Saddam Iraq" within weeks of taking office in early 2001, and an attack on Iraq was "an abiding theme" at practically every National Security Council meeting he attended. The neo-conservatives and hardline nationalists who dominated the Bush administration's foreign policy weren't duped by misleading intelligence; they *manufactured* the misleading intelligence in order to justify an invasion that they had long wanted to pursue for other reasons. What reasons?

The Project for the New American Century was the Bush administration's foreign policy team in embryo, linking ideologically motivated neo-conservatives like Wolfowitz and Feith with tough nationalists like Cheney and Rumsfeld. At the start, only the former lot saw the overthrow of Saddam Hussein as a moral enterprise worth pursuing. Cheney was a pragmatist who defended the first President Bush's decision not to roll on up to Baghdad and overthrow Saddam after liberating Kuwait in the 1991 Gulf War (in which he served as secretary of defence). He told ABC's *This Week* at the time, "I think for us to get American military personnel involved in a civil war inside Iraq would literally be a quagmire. Once we got to Baghdad, what would we do? Who would we put in power? What kind of government? Would it be a Sunni government, a Shia government, a Kurdish government? Would it be secular, along the lines of the Baath Party? Would it be fundamentalist Islamic? I do not think the United States wants to have U.S. military forces accept casualties and accept [the] responsibility of trying to govern Iraq. It makes no sense at all." In terms of PNAC's founding manifesto, which called for a "Reaganite policy of military strength and moral clarity," hardline nationalists like Cheney and Rumsfeld had no problem with the first part, but they would probably have regarded the "moral clarity" part as idealistic drivel.

Nevertheless, the purpose of PNAC was to unite the various strands of radical opinion on the right of the Republican Party in a bid to gain control of the party's foreign policy, so there had to be some flagship policy proposal on which they could all agree. The invasion of Iraq and the overthrow of Saddam Hussein was the one they agreed on.

For the neo-conservatives, Iraq was the ideal target. These were the people, intoxicated by America's apparent success in bringing down the Communist tyrannies of Europe in 1989–91 through that famous combination of "military strength and moral clarity," who wanted to do it again to all the other nasty regimes in the world, starting with the ones that regularly defied the United States. But doing that required supreme, unchallengeable power, so they were equally concerned to consolidate American global hegemony, an asset which had fallen into their laps in 1991 with the collapse of the Soviet Union, but which they felt had been gravely damaged by the indecisiveness and timidity of U.S. foreign policy during the two Clinton administrations. They felt that it was necessary to relaunch *Pax Americana*, the omnipresent though usually unspoken claim that the United States has the right and the duty to impose order and to discipline "bad guys" around the planet, because it is the only country with the power and the moral authority to fulfill that role, and Iraq seemed like the ideal candidate to be the horrible example. The regime was militarily very weak and universally unpopular, and a rapid U.S. military victory, followed by an equally rapid process of economic and political reconstruction, would produce an Iraq whose prosperity and democracy silenced any critics of U.S. unilateralism and disregard for international law. The world would conclude that the implicit U.S. offer to take over the job of world policeman was genuine, reliable, and useful enough to set aside those nagging little doubts about the legality of invading a sovereign state out of the blue.

Iraq was doubly the ideal target for the neo-conservatives because it was seen as the greatest danger to Israel, which Saddam had showered with missiles during the first Gulf War in 1991 – and many of the core neo-conservatives were Zionists who had strong links with the hardline Likud Party in Israel. Paul Wolfowitz, Douglas Feith, Richard Perle, and Elliott Abrams, President Bush's chief adviser on the Middle East, had all served on the staff of Democratic Senator Henry "Scoop"

Jackson in the 1970s, when the latter's main goal in life had been to force the Soviet Union to allow free Jewish emigration to Israel by manipulating U.S. trade laws. Jackson won in the end, and a million Soviet Jews moved to Israel to swell the state's population, but by the end of the 1970s his young aides, frustrated by the politics of compromise, had moved on to a more congenial home in the Republican Party. (Hence "neo"-conservative.) They maintained their close ties with the Likud Party in Israel, and if the destruction of Saddam Hussein's regime would serve Likud's purposes, that was good enough for them.

Settling on Iraq as PNAC's first target was less obvious for the non-Zionists in the new organization, but whereas regime change in Baghdad had not been of interest to most of them in the early 1990s, it became more attractive as the decade neared its end. This had little to do with the good or bad behaviour of Saddam Hussein, and quite a lot to do with the rising importance of China as a potential adversary of the United States. In 1992, the United States had towered above the political landscape like a colossus, with no serious rival in sight. By 2000, it was no longer glad, confident morning; the bad old world of rival great powers was back. The emerging rivals were not nearly powerful enough yet to challenge American power directly, to be sure, but by the later 1990s anybody with access to a pocket calculator could work out when they would reach that point with a fair degree of confidence.

A continuation of China's 10 per cent annual economic growth for forty more years would give the country a gross domestic product equal to that of the United States by about 2040, and economic power is the root of all other kinds of power, including military power. Eight or 9 per cent annual economic growth would give even India the same GDP as the

United States by the late 2040s, give or take a few years, for a developed economy like that of the United States cannot be driven at much more than 4 per cent growth a year. America's tenure as the world's sole superpower was therefore due to expire in about one long generation, unless they could figure out a way to extend the lease.

It doesn't much matter whether this is a true picture of the future or not. Obviously, projections of current trends that run decades into the future are vulnerable to all sorts of historical surprises. The predicted late 2040s world of three superpowers of roughly equivalent strength, China, the United States, and India, is a surprise-free scenario, and at least some major details of the real future are likely to be very different: China could suffer domestic political upheavals that cost it a decade or more of growth (as happened in the 1960s and 1970s); India could lose half a dozen cities in a nuclear war with Pakistan; runaway climate change could make all projections based on current economic models irrelevant. What matters is that the people who would determine U.S. defence and foreign policy in the new Republican administration *believed* in this surprise-free picture of the future, and based their strategic thinking on it.

Of the two emerging Asian giants, China seemed more threatening because it was much closer to the United States, catching up much faster, and, above all, it was a Communist dictatorship whereas India was an increasingly capitalist democracy. From the moment they took office in January 2001, the Bush foreign policy team pursued a policy towards China that came to be called "congagement" in Washington insider slang: political and economic "engagement" with China, a major American trading partner, in the hope that Beijing could be steered into paths acceptable to the United

States, but at the same time "containment," in case it could not. The "containment" part of the strategy, in addition to re-basing U.S. forces in the western Pacific closer to the Chinese coast, involved strengthening old U.S. military alliances and building new ones all around China's borders, and it got a great deal of attention from the White House despite the huge distraction of 9/11 and the "war on terror": large bureaucratic organizations like governments are well suited to multi-tasking.

The two main goals of the new U.S. strategy in Asia were to persuade Japan to cast off the restraints of the "peace" constitution and become a "normal" country with large armed forces capable of being deployed overseas, and to lure India, the other emerging Asian giant, into a military alliance with the United States. Progress in Japan was slow but steady—Japanese troops in Iraq working an "reconstruction" projects, Japanese Navy ships refueling U.S. warships in the Indian Ocean in support of operations in Afghanistan—until the collapse of Prime Minister Shinzo Abe's government in September 2007, but that may mean that the key project to eliminate the "peace" clause from the Japanese constitution is put on hold indefinitely.

The Indian component of Washington's strategy has made more progress. The ten-year U.S.–Indian military co-operation agreement signed in June 2005 is not formally a military alliance, of course, but for many practical purposes it works like one, and a measure of how important it was to the United States is the scale of the concessions that the Indian negotiators were able to extract from Washington: Indian access to the next generation of American military technology (with almost full technology transfer), and full Indian access to American civil nuclear technology and nuclear fuel exports despite the Indian nuclear weapons tests of 1998 that had initially triggered U.S. export embargoes. In the context of this growing American strategic obsession with China, the Middle East also began to grow in strategic importance even in the eyes of the pragmatic nationalists in PNAC, for one of China's great and growing vulnerabilities was its dependence on overseas oil – most of which came from the Persian Gulf.

Wouldn't it be handy if the United States had strong, permanent military bases in the heart of the Gulf region, from which it could at need cut off China's oil imports and strangle its economy? Wouldn't the Chinese behave a whole lot better if they knew that the United States had that ability?

The U.S. military position in the Gulf was currently assured by American bases in Saudi Arabia (negotiated by Dick Cheney himself when he was secretary of defence in 1990), but the Saudis wanted the American soldiers out for fear that their continued presence was destabilizing the kingdom. So why not take down Saddam Hussein, replace him with a compliant and pro-American government, and move the American military bases to Iraq? The neo-conservatives could potter around to their hearts' content with their project for implanting American democratic values in the Arab world (which would, in their imaginations, make Iraqis more kindly disposed towards Israel) and the hardline nationalists would have the permanent military bases in the Gulf from which to prevent any oil reaching China in a crisis. Here was a goal they could all agree on, so it became the trademark policy of PNAC.

"For the neo-conservatives the prime motivation for the invasion of Iraq was to secure a new base for U.S. influence in the region. Donald Rumsfeld and Paul Wolfowitz did not waste time on an exit strategy because they imagined they were going in to Iraq to stay.

"One engaging consequence of their boundless self-confidence is that they were always perfectly open about their goal, and neo-con demands for a new strategic presence for the U.S. can be traced back long before the victory of President Bush. The attack on the Twin Towers sharpened their designs on Iraq, not because there was a scintilla of evidence that Saddam had any connection to it, but because the multiple Saudi links brought home the urgency of identifying an alternative location for U.S. bases. Immediately after the occupation of Iraq, Donald Rumsfeld visited the region to close the U.S. bases in Saudi Arabia that now were thought redundant."

– Robin Cook, British Foreign Secretary, 1997–2001
(Resigned as Leader of the House of Commons in March, 2003
in protest at British participation in the invasion of Iraq)

There are obviously some loose ends in this explanation of how Iraq became the main target of the PNAC crowd, but they can generally be explained by the fact that this policy was much more about the realities in Washington than the realities in Iraq. For example, permanent American military bases in the Gulf were a needless luxury so long as the U.S. Navy could control the mouth of the Gulf in a crisis, so why bother? But then, *most* American military bases overseas are needless luxuries in terms of the country's core strategic requirements. U.S. military spending, currently nearing $600 billion a year, is rather more than that of everybody else in the world put together. With so much money sloshing around, most American strategic solutions (like the famous "Triad" of land-based and submarine-launched missiles plus long-range bombers) tend to be lavish and redundant: belt plus suspenders plus a rope around the waist for good luck.

How could the neo-conservatives have been so confident that

they knew how to transform Arab societies when few of them had ever even been there? That's easy. They were ideological crusaders who were not interested in the specific history and culture of the societies they wanted to change because they were convinced that they had a one-size-fits-all solution that would work anywhere. Bring the Iraqis "American values," even at the point of a gun, and they will eagerly embrace them and turn into an Israel-friendly free-market democracy.

The neo-conservatives and the nationalists who came together to found the Project for the New American Century managed to agree on Iraq as the right place to invade, the former mainly because of their loyalty to Israel and the latter because of their fears about the growing power of China, but why did they want to invade anywhere at all? What was it about the PNAC project that required the United States to invade somewhere and, in effect, make a horrible example of it? The answer will be found in "Rebuilding America's Defenses: Strategy, Forces and Resources for a New Century," the last document produced by PNAC before they all got senior jobs in the new Bush administration and stopped writing for publication.

"Rebuilding America's Defenses" offers a uniquely valuable insight into the beliefs and goals of the men and women who had gathered under the PNAC banner, because it was written before they realized that they were on the brink of gaining control of American foreign and defence policy. A little more than a year before, Condoleezza Rice had given them their opportunity by selecting several of their number to serve on the ad hoc board of policy advisers, nicknamed the "Vulcans," whose task was to help George W. Bush, a contender for the Republican presidential nomination, to formulate a set of policies on foreign affairs and defence. They then got very lucky when Bush selected the most prominent of their number, Dick Cheney, as his vice-presidential candidate. Two months after the report was published in September 2000, Bush would win the presidential election, more or less. By the end of January, thanks largely to Cheney's influence, the leading members of PNAC would effectively be in charge of American foreign and defence policy. But when the PNAC report went off to the printers, probably in June or July 2000, they did not and dared not foresee any of that, and its tone is not in the least triumphal.

In fact, it is not even a rabidly partisan document. The authors of "Rebuilding America's Defenses" took occasional slaps at the Clinton administrations of the 1990s, but they were really addressing the split on foreign policy that had festered within the Republican Party itself since the end of the Cold War. It was George H.W. Bush, the father of their own favoured candidate in the 2000 presidential election, who had forced Dick Cheney to tone down his radical Defense Planning Guidance in 1992, and it was opposition to the senior Bush's multilateralism that united the unilateral nationalists and the crusading neo-conservatives at PNAC. Nor did they expect their proposals to become policy any time in the near future: in Chapter V, they predict that "the process of transformation [of American defence policy] . . . is likely to be a long one, absent some catastrophic and catalyzing event – like a new Pearl Harbor." The authors of the report were still outsiders trying to make a case, and so they laid it out in painstaking detail.

The context for their analysis was stated in the bluntest possible terms in the introduction to the report: "The United States is the world's only superpower, combining preeminent military power, global technological leadership, and the world's largest economy. . . . At present the United States faces no global rival.

America's grand strategy should aim to preserve and extend this advantageous position as far into the future as possible. . . ." Thus far, at least, they would have found virtually no American strategic thinker, military or civilian, who disagreed with them. But as soon as they delved into the details of force structure, equipment acquisitions, and the weapons technology needed to "extend this advantageous position into the future," the consensus fell away, for they wanted a much bigger defence budget even than the ones during the Cold War era.

There is a disarming directness in the brisk way that the study's authors reopen the battle that Cheney's Defense Department lost to the elder Bush's White House in 1992: "In broad terms, we saw the project as building upon the defense strategy outlined by the Cheney Defense Department in the waning days of the [elder] Bush administration. The Defense Planning Guidance drafted in the early months of 1992 provided a blueprint for maintaining U.S. preeminence, precluding the rise of a great power rival, and shaping the international security order in line with American principles and interests. . . . [Eight years later] the basic tenets of the DPG, in our judgment, remain sound." The target audience here is both the grandees and the base of the Republican Party. By 2000, the unilateralists and hardline nationalists within the party had largely succeeded in wresting control of policy away from the people around the senior Bush who still believed in multilateralism, diplomacy, and international institutions, but their victory was neither complete nor secure and so the struggle continued.

And what was the geographical focus of their concerns? The Gulf gets due attention: "In the Persian Gulf region, the presence of American forces . . . has become a semi-permanent fact of life. . . . Indeed, the United States has for decades sought to play a more permanent role in Gulf regional security. While the unresolved conflict with Iraq provides the immediate justification, the need for a substantial American force presence in the Gulf transcends the issue of the regime of Saddam Hussein." But the real focus is the rise of China, which will necessitate the repositioning of U.S. forces and the cultivation of new U.S. allies in Asia. On page two of the report is a little table that neatly summarizes the shift in U.S. strategy that they are advocating:

	Cold War	21st Century
Security system	Bipolar	Unipolar
Strategic goal	Contain Soviet Union	Preserve *Pax Americana*
Main military mission(s)	Deter Soviet expansionism	Secure and expand zones of democratic peace; deter rise of new great-power competitor; defend key regions; exploit transformation of war
Main military threat(s)	Potential global war across many theaters	Potential theater wars spread across globe
Focus of strategic competition	Europe	East Asia

The Middle East doesn't even warrant a mention in this schematic, because in purely strategic terms it simply wasn't a big issue for the PNAC strategists. China was the big threat on which they think American strategy must focus. Yet it was Iraq that the same people actually wanted to invade. They had publicly advocated invading it ever since early 1998, and as soon as they got into office they set the wheels in motion for the invasion. Make sense of that.

Pretty well everyone at the PNAC wanted to invade somewhere and take down some unpopular/dangerous/nasty regime. They all understood that the greatest "force multiplier" for a great power is a reputation for ruthless determination and military success, and they were all concerned that the Clinton years had damaged that U.S. reputation: "As we have seen," says the 2000 document, "even a small failure like that in Somalia or a halting and incomplete triumph as in the Balkans can cast doubt on American credibility." They all agreed that any new administration that wanted to turn this situation around and restore the credibility of *Pax Americana* would need to give the world a striking demonstration of its irresistible power. So whom should they invade?

For the neo-conservative minority, most of whom were also Likudniks, the choice was obvious: Iraq. The hardline nationalists and unilateralists who were not Zionists were not similarly dedicated to any particular target, but agreed on the need for some dramatic action, and Iraq recommended itself to them as an ideal target for invasion for three reasons. First, it was already an established bogeyman in the minds of the American public, which would make it easier to persuade them that an invasion was necessary. Second, it was a potential base from which the United States could permanently dominate the entire Persian Gulf and, at need, deny the oil of the region to China. And third, Saddam Hussein's regime was so weak and isolated militarily and in every other way that an invasion would be certain to succeed, at a very low cost in American casualties.

It will never be proven that this was the logic by which Iraq became PNAC's preferred invasion target, because shredders are universal nowadays and the really sensitive stuff gets dealt with on the phone or in person. But there has to be some logical reason why Iraq was on their hit list years before 9/11 came along and gave them a publicly defensible pretext for invading the place (if you cooked the intelligence just right), and this is the only one that makes sense. So now that their splendid adventure is collapsing around their ears, what can all this analysis of their motives for invading Iraq in the first place tell us about future American policy in the region?

Quite a lot, actually. It tells us that the "neo-conservatives" were not so indispensable to the decision to invade Iraq as they seemed at the time. It also tells us that while the broad strategic concerns of the traditional nationalists within PNAC and the Bush administration will doubtless continue to shape U.S. foreign policy in various ways, the main focus of those concerns is not the Middle East.

9/11 brought the neo-conservatives to the fore in the Bush administration, since the standard American explanation for the actions of the terrorists emphasized the alleged conflict of "values" (as in President Bush's endless assertions that "they hate our values"), while dismissing any suggestion that the terrorists might be largely driven by concrete historical and contemporary grievances about American policy in the Middle East. The neo-conservatives claimed that they had the key with which to transform Arab society – American military and ideological power will democratize it, and that automatically de-radicalizes it – so they were pushed out front and told to get on with it. But they would never have persuaded the White House to invade Iraq just to democratize it. Their promises of political and social transformation proved to be empty, and they stand little chance of recapturing the American imagination for the foreseeable future. Failure on that scale leaves indelible lessons: there will be no further U.S. military enterprises based on the assumption of a "democratic transition" in the target society for a long time to come.

The strategic motives of the less ideological majority among the PNAC alumni – impressing the world with the military might and determination of the United States, and/or getting a stranglehold on China's sources of raw materials – may well reappear in one form or another in the foreign policy of future American administrations, for the United States will probably continue to struggle against the fate of demotion to the status of just one more great power. But it is not inevitable, or even very likely, that the Middle East will be the venue for future dramas of this sort. The inexorable shift of strategic attention to the Asia-Pacific region will continue, and China's vulnerability to blackmail strategies like the one that partly lay behind the U.S. invasion of Iraq will decrease as it diversifies its sources of oil and shifts the traffic from tankers to overland pipelines.

In sum, the U.S. invasion of Iraq was not primarily driven by Middle Eastern considerations at all, and its principal long-term effect may be to clarify for the next generation of American policy-makers the quite limited extent to which American interests are involved in the Middle East. The gradual emergence of China as a great-power challenger to the United States, and the American alliance-building in Asia that it has triggered, will continue to shift U.S. attention away from the Middle East, so the various upheavals within the region that follow the final American retreat from Iraq are likely to unfold without strenuous U.S. intervention. Only a direct military attack on Iran by the United States would substantially change that conclusion – and even then, one suspects, the subsequent crisis would delay the U.S. exit from the region by only a few years.

Like most silver linings, this one comes concealed in some very dark storm-clouds, and some people have already paid a very high price for it: the Iraqis.

CHAPTER III

THE THREAT TO THE OLD ORDER

"I do know we have not succeeded as fast as we hoped. . . . I am disappointed by the pace of success."

– President George W. Bush, Washington, December 7, 2006

"We will beat them when we realise that it's not our fault that they're doing this. We will win if we don't apologise for our values."

– Prime Minister Tony Blair, London, February 21, 2007

It's hard to know what to call this strange period when the American and British invasion of Iraq has clearly failed, but the men who ordered the invasion have not yet admitted failure and the consequences of their failure have not yet become clear. "Twilight of the Dwarves," perhaps? At any rate, it will last for some time yet, because the war in Iraq is essentially a guerrilla struggle against a foreign occupation, and guerrilla wars normally end only when the (militarily superior) foreigners accept that the war is unwinnable, cut their losses, and go home.

Bush's admission that "I am disappointed by the pace of success" sounds a bit like Emperor Hirohito's concession, in his broadcast after the atomic bomb destroyed Hiroshima, that "the war has developed not necessarily to Japan's advantage." The man must be in agony inside, for the war that was going to be a "cakewalk" has turned into a monster that is devouring his presidency and his reputation. Yet he cannot simply quit and walk away from Iraq without at least some fleeting semblance of success: too many Americans have died for him just to admit that it was all a mistake and say he's sorry.

The "surge" of American troops in Iraq that began early in 2007 was aimed at creating a period of relative stability that would allow the United States to declare a victory and leave – or at least remove most of its combat troops – in mid-2008, in time to produce a positive effect for the Republican Party in the presidential elections next November. The odds on that period of stability actually happening, however, are poor, and without it no major withdrawal of U.S. troops from Iraq is likely before Bush leaves office. They will have to stay so that he does not have to admit that the whole Iraq adventure was a blunder and a waste.

The situation in Britain is somewhat different. Tony Blair watched his whole ten-year prime ministership and his reputation being devoured by the monster he helped to create in Iraq, and he sometimes seemed quite unhinged by it. (What, for example, could he have meant by "We will beat them when we realise that it's not our fault that they're doing this"? That victory over the Iraqi insurgency will come when the British people realize that they are blameless, and that it's the Iraqis' own fault for resisting?) But no British prime minister has the unchallengeable power of an American president, and the mounting discomfort of Blair's cabinet colleagues, even those who originally supported the war, played a big part in forcing him to leave office in mid-2007.

Even before that, he was compelled to announce in February 2007 a timetable of sorts for the withdrawal of British troops from southern Iraq, in order not to burden his successor as Labour Party leader with the full blame for the needless, lost war. However, it looked bad for the British to be leaving Iraq just as the Americans are "surging," so out of consideration for his senior partner in Washington, Blair announced a very drawn-out process of disengagement that would leave most of the British troops in Iraq until sometime in 2008 (while getting them off the dangerous streets of the southern city of Basra a lot sooner). That timetable may accelerate sharply now that Gordon Brown is safely in office.

Most of the other members of the "coalition" who were cajoled, bullied, or bribed into sending troops to Iraq have already gone home, or are in the process of leaving. By early 2008, more than 95 per cent of the foreign troops in Iraq will be American. By early 2009, when the next American president takes office, they will almost certainly all be called home too – unless, of course, there is another large-scale terrorist attack on the United States. That might conceivably change things, though it is far from certain.

Another major terrorist attack on U.S. soil, killing at least hundreds of Americans, if not the thousands of 9/11, is a permanent possibility, but it is a pretty remote one. However, another al-Qaeda attack on the United States might stampede Americans back into the arms of those who insist that the war in Iraq is part of the "global war on terror," so the Islamist organization (or what remains of it) will doubtless be trying to make that happen.

It is certainly in al-Qaeda's interest to keep American troops pinned down in Iraq, where their presence and their behaviour serve to radicalize people throughout the Arabic and the broader Islamic world: American soldiers have long been al-Qaeda's best recruiters. But it is doubtful that al-Qaeda or any other foreign-based outfit has the capacity to carry out a major terrorist attack in the United States in the face of much-improved surveillance. Homegrown attacks by disaffected American Muslims, on the pattern of the London bombings of July 2005, are a different matter, but the level of risk in the United States may be significantly lower as Muslim immigrants to the U.S. are generally considered to be more fully integrated into the general American culture than those in most European countries. And in any case, a *homegrown* terrorist attack might not be of much use in persuading Americans that keeping troops in Iraq makes them safer from terrorism than pulling them out.

The other imponderable in the present situation is the possibility of an American attack on Iran, a decision that lies in the hands of one man. The forces are in place to do the job, and journalist Seymour Hersh of *The New Yorker* reported in February 2007 that the White House had asked the Pentagon for a plan of attack that could be implemented within twenty-four hours of the word *go*. The temptation to play double or nothing must be very strong for President Bush, in the sense that things are so bad already, from a "legacy" point of view, that attacking Iran can't make them worse, and might at least change the context in which the administration is being judged. Roll the dice.

"I don't know how many times the president, secretary [of state Condoleezza] Rice, and I have had to repeat that we have no intention of attacking Iran."
— Secretary of Defense Robert Gates,
quoted in *The Guardian*, February 10, 2007

"Planning is going on, in spite of public disavowals by Gates. Targets have been selected. For a bombing campaign against nuclear sites, it is quite advanced. The military assets to carry this out are being put in place. We are planning for war. It is incredibly dangerous."
— Vincent Cannistraro, founder, IntelligenceBrief

Vincent Cannistraro is a twenty-seven-year CIA veteran who served as Director for Intelligence Programs at the National Security Agency under President Reagan, chaired the Afghanistan Working Group at the White House, and worked as Special Assistant for Intelligence in the office of the Secretary of Defense. He has been around the block several times and he has got his hands dirty: for part of the 1980s, he was the CIA's main contact with the "Contra" guerrillas who were seeking to overthrow the Sandinista government in Nicaragua. He now runs a private security and intelligence business, IntelligenceBrief, for a largely corporate clientele. If he says that planning for an American war against Iran is well advanced, it would be a good idea to listen.

The United States can't actually invade Iran on the ground, because after four years of occupying Iraq and six years in Afghanistan most of its ground-combat troops are in one of those countries, or just back from a tour in one of those countries, or training to return for another tour in one of them. But Washington could bomb Iran as much and as long as it wants with relative impunity, for Iranian air defences cannot cope with state-of-the-art American technology. And Vice President Dick Cheney keeps growling that "all options are on the table" so far as Iran is concerned.

He may well mean it, for the extreme lame-duck status of the administration liberates it from all the political considerations that would normally restrain it. President Bush is forbidden by law, and Cheney by the state of his health, from running for re-election, so it no longer matters to them if what they do is unpopular. The Republican Party might be made to pay for the attack at the next election, but even that is not a foregone conclusion – particularly if the attack took place quite close to the vote in November 2008, so that the vote was held in an atmosphere of crisis and superheated patriotism.

Many people assume that Bush and Cheney, having invaded Iraq illegally and on false pretences, having bungled the occupation so badly that a large majority of Iraqis now approve of attacks on U.S. troops, and having lost almost four thousand American soldiers killed and eight or nine times that number seriously wounded, are now in a very weak position politically, but that's not how it works. With nothing to look forward to but impending defeat and humiliation if events continue on their present course, they have every incentive to roll the dice one more time – and so long as their military chiefs remain willing to obey their orders, they can still do just that. It would be messy, though.

Since Iran's nuclear facilities are widely dispersed, and in some cases deeply buried, it would take many hundreds of air strikes, perhaps even some thousands, to do major damage to the country's uranium-enrichment program, plus many more to suppress Iranian air defences. Thousands of Iranians would be killed, for many of the nuclear facilities are in urban areas, and the United States would almost certainly time the attack during working hours in order to kill the maximum number of the nuclear specialists who work in those facilities. There might be some radiation release, which would compound the damage. There is even wild talk in some U.S. military circles about using "mini-nukes" to dig out sites that are so deep, like those at Arak and Natanz, that they may not be vulnerable to ordinary bombs. (This would cross the "nuclear firebreak" for the first time since 1945, and no nuclear weapons are really "mini"; the smallest are dozens of times more powerful than the biggest conventional bombs.)

But then, after only a few days, the United States would have shot its bolt. Apart from a blockade of Iran's ports, there is nothing more that it could do to the country except to carry out some more air raids. Whereas there is a great deal that Iran could do in retaliation.

"We do not want to use the oil weapon. It is them who would impose it on us . . . [but] we will react in a way that would be painful for them. Do not force us to do something that will make people shiver in the cold."
– Ali Larijani, Iran's chief nuclear negotiator and secretary of the Supreme National Security Council, August 6, 2006

Iran could flood U.S.-occupied Iraq with advanced weaponry for penetrating American armoured vehicles and downing U.S. bombers. It could encourage the Shia militias in Iraq that are closely aligned with Iran – mainly the Badr Brigade, the armed wing of the Supreme Council for the Islamic Revolution in Iraq (SCIRI) – to attack American troops, thus giving the U.S. Army a formidable new enemy in Iraq. As for the British troops who still allegedly hold southern Iraq, an American general told *New Yorker* journalist Seymour Hersh in 2006 that the Iranians could take Basra with "ten mullahs and a sound truck."

Iran could stop its own oil exports entirely, thus panicking the oil markets around the world and driving up prices. It would also stand a fair chance of being able to shut down *all* oil-tanker traffic in and out of the Persian Gulf, thus cutting off between a quarter and a third of the world's oil supply. The Iranian navy is no match for the U.S. Navy, but it doesn't need to be. Its fast attack boats, minelayers, and diesel submarines could sink enough tankers to drive shipping insurance rates prohibitively high, and for the longer haul its shore-based sea-skimming missiles, with enough range to cover the whole Persian Gulf and the Gulf of Oman, can be launched from several thousand kilometres of coastline. Sink even one tanker a week, and the Gulf stays closed. So does much of the world's economy.

Iran also has political options that terrify much of the nearby Arab world, for many of these countries contain large Shia minorities – in Lebanon, where the Shias are concentrated in the south, near the border with Israel; in Saudi Arabia, where they comprise around half the population in the Eastern Province (where all the oil is), and in several of the smaller Gulf sheikhdoms. In most cases, the Shias are the poorest community in the country, and there is often a history of discrimination or persecution as well, so Iran could, if it wished, use propaganda, secret subsidies, and agents provocateurs to stir up serious trouble between the regimes and their Shia subjects. That could make things very difficult for the United States and its friends in the region.

How long could Iran hold out in such a confrontation with the United States, where it faced a naval blockade and air raids but no threat of actual land invasion? For quite some time, probably, since an unprovoked American attack on Iran would generate a wave of patriotic fervour and social solidarity among ordinary Iranians that would make it easier for the regime to ride out an extended period of economic privation. Meanwhile, the rest of the Muslim world would be mobilizing against local American interests as never before, for it would inevitably see the onslaught on Iran as part of a larger American onslaught against Islam itself. As Oscar Wilde almost said, for America to invade one Muslim country may be seen as merely unfortunate, but to invade two looks like carelessness. To attack a *third* would definitely smack of malice aforethought.

"I think of war with Iran as the ending of America's present role in the world. . . . Iraq may have been a preview of that, but it's still redeemable if we get out fast. In a war with Iran, we'll get dragged down for twenty or thirty years. The world will condemn us. We will lose our position in the world."

– Zbigniew Brzezinski, former national security adviser, interview by David Ignatius in *The Washington Post*, April 12, 2006

What would American attacks on Iran achieve? *If* Iran's uranium-enrichment program is intended to produce nuclear weapons, which is a lot less certain than the White House's propaganda would have us believe – these are the same people who assured us that Saddam Hussein had weapons of mass destruction, after all – then the sort of air strikes that the United States can carry out would set the program back a couple of years at most. And since everybody agrees that Iran is still five to ten years away from being able to build an actual nuclear bomb, including both the latest National Intelligence Estimate of the U.S. government and Mohamed ElBaradei, director general of the International Atomic Energy Agency (IAEA), it's hard to see what the rush is. Yet many experienced and well-informed people worry that an administration that talked itself into believing that invading Iraq was a good idea is perfectly capable of making the same sort of mistake with Iran.

If Bush & Co. did decide on such a gamble, Congress could not move fast enough to stop them. Neither could America's friends and allies, because Washington wouldn't tell them its plans in advance, and doesn't pay much heed to their views anyway. America's professional soldiers have an implicit duty to protect the republic from the consequences of such a monumental military folly, and many of them are well aware of the grave consequences of an unprovoked attack on Iran, but there is little precedent in the United States for senior officers to resign in protest against a disastrously wrong strategy. In practical terms, President Bush is as free to order an attack on Iran today as he was to order the invasion of Iraq in 2003. The price, in terms of America's position in the world, would be every bit as great as Brzezinski suggests.

If the United States attacked Iran, most European countries would be scrambling to dissociate themselves from the American action, and it could even spell the end of the NATO alliance (some twenty years after it outlived its original purpose). For the Russians, it would be the final evidence that the United States is a reckless country whose actions can only be constrained by counterbalancing force, and that conclusion could push them into a military understanding with the Chinese. All this would be happening, moreover, in a world that was in the grip of the worst economic crisis for at least forty years for lack of oil. It would be a memorable year, and at the end of it America's power in the world would be greatly diminished. An American attack on Iran would alter the political landscape almost everywhere – except, curiously, in the Middle East.

Attacking Iran would hasten and deepen the general American retreat from the region that is already the likeliest consequence of defeat in Iraq, but it would not lead to radically different outcomes. After some months, a way would doubtless be found to extricate the United States diplomatically from an unwinnable war with Iran and to reopen the Persian Gulf to tanker traffic, but it would certainly entail the removal of all U.S. military bases in the Persian Gulf, notably in Bahrain and Qatar. Even if the Iranians could not themselves insist on such a concession, the local regimes would have to do so in order to curry favour with the new paramount power in the region and to placate their own significant Shia populations. It is quite likely that Arab regimes even farther afield (and lacking any Shia minority) would also demand the removal of American bases and troops in response to aroused anti-American sentiment among their own people.

As for Iraq itself, a U.S. attack on Iran would certainly drive the Shia-dominated government in Baghdad into a closer relationship with its giant Shia neighbour, at least for a while, but it would not substantially change the range of possible outcomes for Iraq after U.S. troops leave. At best, Iraq will fall far short of being the beacon of democracy and prosperity that the American neo-conservatives fondly imagined they were creating, and at worst it could just break up into three warring states. It is the latter possibility that prompts apocalyptic visions in which Iraq becomes the solvent that dissolves the entire existing order in the region.

The Arab states will be sucked into this Iraqi maelstrom. With the world's only superpower on its way out, who but they – along with Turkey and Iran – are left to replace it there? But they will fail disastrously in their turn. . . . In fact almost all these countries are latent Iraqs, especially Ba'athist Syria. Far from mastering Iraq, it is Iraq – in its death throes as a unified state – that is more likely to master them. Nor will Turkey and Iran, Iraq's strongest neighbours, be immune from

the contagion, with Iraqi Kurdish emancipation already contributing
to a resurgence of Kurdish resistance in both.

– David Hirst, *The Guardian*, January 13, 2006

It is a hellish vision of the future, with borders shifting and entire states falling apart as the Iraqi "contagion" unleashed by the 2003 invasion spreads across the region. The big winner at the state level would be Iran, but the real winners right across the Arab world at the ideological level would be the Islamist fanatics who already dominate both the Shia and the Sunni sides in the Iraqi civil war. The old order already seems almost helpless before the ruthless energy of the extremists. As Saudi Arabia's foreign minister, Prince Saud al-Faisal, said at a September 2005 press conference, explaining why he would not appoint an ambassador to Baghdad: "I doubt that he'd last a day." (Both the Egyptian and the Algerian ambassadors to Iraq were kidnapped and murdered in mid-2005.)

When a man like David Hirst coolly predicts the collapse of the entire political order that he has reported on for most of his life – he was the *Guardian*'s Middle East correspondent from 1963 until 2001 – you have to take him seriously. Hirst is all in favour of a general U.S. retreat from the region, which he sees as "a prerequisite for . . . the emergence of a healthy, self-reliant new Middle Eastern order," but he is convinced that a "bad" U.S. retreat involving an ignominious scuttle from Iraq will unleash boundless jihadi violence and drive the existing regimes to "even cruder methods – increased internal repression or external adventurism – to preserve themselves." And there is plenty of wild talk by officials that suggests that things are indeed drifting rapidly in that direction.

Thus, for example, Nawaf Obaid, a security adviser at the Saudi Arabian embassy in Washington, who told the *Washington Post* in December 2006 that "One of the first consequences [of a U.S. withdrawal from Iraq] will be massive Saudi intervention to stop Iranian-backed Shi'ite militias from butchering Iraqi Sunnis." Obaid was fired a week later, and the Saudi Arabian government officially denied his remarks, but there is little doubt that such measures are being discussed in Riyadh. Thus also the warnings by King Abdullah of Jordan that the Middle East faces a cold war, or even a hot one, between what he has dubbed the "Shia crescent" and the Sunni Arab states to the south. Some Jordanian politicians have even spoken of the need to build a "Sunni wall" within Iraq to contain the Shia threat.

"If the Arab states don't come to our help, they will find [Iran] at their gate. For the sake of the entire Muslim community worldwide, the beast has to be destroyed in Iraq."

– Mohammed Bashar al-Faidi, spokesman for the
Association of [Sunni] Muslim Scholars in Iraq,
quoted in *Time* magazine, February 22, 2007

There are those in Washington who eagerly repeat these predictions, presumably because they believe that any Arab war (cold or hot) between the "Shia crescent" and the leading Sunni Arab states to the south (Saudi Arabia, Jordan, and Egypt, all America's allies already), would provide an opportunity for the United States to reassert its dominant position in the region. Even if this were true, it would be a particularly shameless strategy, exploiting the mess that the United States has created by its past blunders to justify a new role as the protector of conservative Sunni states against militant, expansionist Shia ones, but it is not true.

Iran, to be sure, is about 90 per cent Shia, and already has great influence among the Shias of Iraq, who comprise about 60 per cent of the population there. But even in the case of Iraq and Iran, their shared Shia identity only sometimes outweighs the quite different languages and histories of the two communities: it is most unlikely that a Shia-dominated government in Baghdad would subordinate itself to the regime of the ayatollahs in Tehran. And the rest of the "crescent" is mere fantasy.

Syria has been dominated for almost forty years by an Alawi minority who are technically Shia, and who account for only about 10 per cent of the population, but their clan and religious ties have been carefully hidden behind the facade of the local Ba'ath Party. They are unlikely to be so foolish as to alienate the great majority of Syrians, who are Sunni, by openly putting the country on the Shia side of a Sunni–Shia confrontation – because if they did, they would quickly lose power. As for Lebanon, where Shias are the largest single group in the ethnic and sectarian patchwork quilt of that country but well short of a majority, a generalized Shia–Sunni conflict across the region would simply result in a reopening of the Lebanese civil war. There is also a Shia minority in Turkey, especially in the southeast, but Turkey is a secular, semi-developed state that would never allow itself to become entangled in a religious quarrel between Arabs and Persians.

The Sunni–Shia violence that is now tormenting Iraq will have repercussions elsewhere in the Arab world, but it is most unlikely to cause the wholesale realignment of the Middle East along a sectarian axis, let alone a full-scale Sunni–Shia war. And if that doesn't happen, then the United States has no prospective new role in the region as the protector of the Sunnis. There is no Plan B, and even if there were, the administration in Washington would not have the popular support at home to carry it out. The United States really has lost this war, and it really is going to have to leave.

What happens next may not be pretty, especially in the initial stages, for change in a region that has been politically frozen for so long can be violent and even vengeful. One or more Arab countries may fall under Islamist control, while other regimes shift their policies sharply in that direction with the goal of warding off revolutionary change: it will not be possible to unwind the consequences of fifty years of constant Western meddling in the affairs of the Arab countries without some upheavals. But it is unlikely that the very heavens will fall, because Arabs are not (as so much Western analysis implicitly suggests) excitable children.

There will be no single, radical Arab superstate run by bearded fanatics whose sole goal is the destruction of the West. Indeed, anti-Western terrorism is likely to decline over time. There will be no war across the Gulf between Iran and its Arab neighbours to the south after a U.S. withdrawal from the region: these states all depend on the oil that flows out to the world in highly vulnerable tankers and pipelines, and they will not kill the goose that lays the golden eggs. There will not even be a united Arab front that is finally capable of taking Israel on militarily as an equal, or at least not for a long while – long enough for Israel to absorb the shock of American withdrawal, adjust its strategy accordingly, and perhaps even achieve a general peace settlement with the Arabs if it moves fast enough. The U.S. defeat in Iraq will leave a very large mess behind, but it isn't the end of the world.

CHAPTER IV

THE FUTURE OF IRAQ

"Every great work of art goes through messy phases while it is in transition. A lump of clay can become a sculpture. Blobs of paint become paintings which inspire. The final test of our efforts will not be the isolated incidents that you report daily, but the country that the Iraqis build."

– Major General William Caldwell,
chief U.S. military spokesman, Baghdad, November 2006

"We need a long-lasting surge because we have to keep in mind that we face an enemy here that adapts to our strategy. If we do a short surge they will just wait us out. We need to surge for at least eighteen months."

– Frederick Kagan, resident scholar at the
American Enterprise Institute, joint author with
General Jack Keane of the "surge" strategy,
interview in *The Observer*, January 17, 2007

President Bush's desire for one last roll of the dice is understandable, and the notion of a "surge" (much nicer word than "escalation," that, if a bit less evocative) was not inherently foolish. But the extra 30,000 American troops he has sent to Iraq amounted to a mere 23 per cent increase in U.S. strength there. If 132,000 U.S. troops could not deliver "victory" in Iraq (in a war that has now lasted longer than American participation in the Second World War), then 162,000 American troops were not likely to do so either. Indeed, the total number of U.S. troops in Iraq was actually higher than that at the end of 2005, and it didn't make the slightest bit of difference.

It's a pathetic escalation, nothing like the huge leap from 50,000 to 550,000 U.S. troops in Vietnam in only three years in 1965–68. Not that that helped the United States to win the Vietnam War in the end – it was probably as unwinnable as the Iraq war from the start – but now the option of major escalation does not even exist, for the U.S. Army is only half the size it was in the 1960s and Bush lacks the political strength to bring back the draft. So it's not surprising that Bush replaced both General George Casey, the commander in Iraq, and General John Abizaid, the head of Central Command (which oversees the entire operation), before he unveiled his "new strategy." Those officers had already privately questioned the usefulness of a "surge" in U.S. troop numbers, and only new leaders, seduced by the promise of promotion and a more senior job, would accept the responsibility for trying to make such a threadbare military policy work.

Another problem with the "surge" was that it reinforced the suspicion of many Shias that the United States was still planning to stay in Iraq permanently, but the greatest worry was that the extra American troops might be primarily intended to take on Moqtada al-Sadr's Mahdi Army, the most violently anti-American of the Shia militias, on home grand. That would have been a very ambitious undertaking if the Mahdi fighters stood their ground. "I don't think [U.S. troops] can dig the Mahdi Army out of Sadr City without levelling it, like Fallujah," counter-insurgency expert Dr. Toby Dodge of the International Institute for Strategic Studies told the *Independent* on April 17, 2007, and using American firepower to level a 2-million-strong Shia slum in Baghdad could finally drive Iraq's other 16 million Shias to revolt.

For those who are haunted by that Famous Final Scene on the roof of the U.S. Embassy in Saigon in 1975, with the desperate crowds of collaborators fighting for seats on the last helicopters out, that is the one route that might deliver the United States to that destination. The Sunni Arab insurgency could eventually drive the U.S. Army out of Iraq by a long process of attrition, but the U.S. withdrawal, when it came, would be a measured and orderly process. If the Shias who make up 60 per cent of the country's population should ever rise up against Americans en masse, it would be a very different story, for they sit astride the long U.S. supply lines all the way up from Kuwait – and a really serious American assault on al-Sadr's stronghold in Sadr City might do the trick. In the event, however, the Mahdi fighters went to ground and Moqtada al-Sadr himself simply disappeared for several months. No need for a showdown with the Americans now: everybody knows that there's less than two years to wait.

Assuming that there is no apocalyptic Battle of Sadr City, it is quite likely that things will just go gradually from bad to somewhat worse across most of Arab Iraq during the period between now and the American withdrawal. The ethnic cleansing has tipped many of the mixed Sunni–Shia areas in Baghdad decisively one way or the other, and most of the smaller pockets of Sunnis or Shias stranded in areas dominated by the other sect have been eliminated entirely, but the Sunnis, who account for around 30 per cent of the capital's population, still hold much of the western and southern suburbs. The Sunni offensive to encircle Baghdad by seizing control of the mixed towns in the farthest outskirts of the capital like Balad and Mahmudiyah succeeded for a time, but it could not cut Shia Baghdad off from the southern Shia hinterland permanently. Kurdistan may continue to get away without any fighting, or it might stumble into a war with Arab Iraq over Kirkuk. Mosul City and province may well split into Arab- and Kurdish-majority areas. Everybody, including the American troops who have been left in the middle of this mess, will have a miserable time, another million or so people will flee their homes, and one or two thousand more American soldiers and many tens of thousands more Iraqis will be killed. Then, by 2009 or 2010, the American troops will all be gone, and we will find out whether there is still an Iraq of some sort.

Time for the analogies. It is true that Baghdad today is like Beirut at the height of the Lebanese civil war in 1975–90: the militias are splitting Baghdad into a dozen different cities, and

Sunni and Shia neighbourhoods that have lived peacefully side
by side since they were built are now exchanging mortar fire
each night. But the civil war in Lebanon finally ended, and all
the Lebanese still co-exist within the same borders – less
happily than before, perhaps, but if they can avoid doing it
again even the deepest wounds will eventually heal. It is not a
foregone conclusion that Iraq must break up, either.

One of the things non-Arabs fail to understand about Iraq,
because of all the intellectual baggage they bring to it from the
various Balkan conflicts of the 1990s, is that there is the same
degree of ethnic and religious diversity in Iraq, but no history
of Balkan-style pogroms. The downtrodden Shia majority
nursed their sense of injustice down the generations, but they
were never targeted for mass killing until they rebelled against
Saddam Hussein at Bush Sr.'s urging, and they didn't even
exploit his overthrow to take vengeance on the Sunni minority. They just set out to demand their fair share of power
through the ballot box.

What finally pitched the Shias and the Sunnis into open war
was their different responses to the American occupation.
Neither community likes the American presence in their
country: a series of opinion polls carried out in Iraq in
September 2006 by the U.S.-based group WorldPublic-
Opinion.org showed that 92 per cent of Sunni Arabs and 62 per
cent of Shias (up from 41 per cent the year before) approved of
attacks on U.S.-led forces. But Shias don't actually carry out
many attacks, because they can see that going along with the
Americans for a little while will give them a democratic system
that finally guarantees them the power that their numbers
warrant. To a Sunni ex-army officer active in the resistance, a
Shia who takes that position is not just a member of another

sect of Islam; he is a collaborator with the enemy and a traitor to his country. It is above all the presence of foreign troops that turns Iraqis against one another and makes the government illegitimate in the eyes of many of its citizens – so the departure of those foreign troops might change the situation.

Not *will* change it, just might, but it is an encouraging thought. Perhaps the blood-curdling predictions in the Baker-Hamilton report will not come to pass after all.

"Other countries in the region fear significant violence crossing their borders. Chaos in Iraq could lead those countries to intervene to protect their own interests. . . . [T]hey fear the distinct possibility of Sunni-Shia clashes across the Islamic world. . . . Such a broader sectarian conflict could open a Pandora's box of problems – including the radicalization of populations, mass movements of populations, and regime changes – that might take decades to play out. . . . A chaotic Iraq could provide a still stronger base of operations for terrorists who seek to act regionally or even globally."

– Iraq Study Group report, December 6, 2006

Maybe the Iraqis, left alone at last, might just get on with the task of rebuilding their country after twenty-four years of Saddam Hussein and six or seven years of American military occupation. By then, tragically, the consequences of the ethnic cleansing that is now raging will have made it much simpler to divide the country up into groups of provinces that are more or less homogeneous from an ethnic and sectarian point of view. Kurdistan is already there, an eight-province "confeder-acy" in the Shia south is gradually sliding into existence, and one Sunni body, the Mujahedin Shura, has already come out in favour of a six-province Sunni Arab region in the west and northwest. Three big cities, Baghdad, Mosul, and Kirkuk, would probably still be home to several groups when the shooting stopped (although they would be living in more clearly defined districts than before), but that anomaly could be dealt with by declaring them special zones but attaching them for financial and legal purposes to the provincial grouping with which the local urban majority shares a language or sect: Baghdad with the Shia confederacy, Mosul with the Sunni western provinces, and Kirkuk with Kurdistan.

The constitution to regulate all this, as it happens, is already in existence, for the basic law that the Iraqis ratified in the 2005 referendum is the most radically decentralized constitution in the known world. It imagines that these regional groupings of provinces, yet to be negotiated and defined, are already in existence, and makes them self-governing in everything except foreign affairs and external defence. It is the regions that would collect taxes, maintain internal security, and make the laws, so if the Shias want sharia law and the Kurds want a secular system, they can happily go their separate ways. For the same reason, there is no protection for women's rights in the constitution: oppress them or not, as your religious or cultural values dictate. Almost all of the 115 brigades in the new army, as well as the police, are recruited mainly from a specific ethnic group and operate exclusively in their own region, and under the 2005 constitution these forces would be answerable first and foremost to the government of their own region.

And there is one big carrot in the constitution for the Sunni Arabs, who have few producing oil fields on their territory. All revenues from existing oil fields will be distributed evenly across all provinces, including those without any oil of their own, in strict proportion to their share of the current total population. (Revenues from fields developed in the future will accrue exclusively to the region where they are located, but even the Sunnis could win that lottery, as there has been little exploration for oil as yet in western Iraq.) Legislation turning this constitutional provision into detailed legal obligations was unanimously approved by Nouri al-Maliki's cabinet in February 2007, although it has yet to be enacted by parliament. It was, by all accounts, primarily the work of U.S. ambassador Zalmay Khalilzad (since replaced), but the point is that Iraqi parties of all groups are willing to support it.

Like most people, Iraqis have always had multiple identities – ethnic, religious, linguistic, professional, tribal or clan (pick any three) – but for both Sunni and Shia Arabs their national identity as Iraqis has always been very strong too. It doesn't die that easily, and they have some very strong economic incentives to renew their membership in a transformed and much less confining Iraqi state when the occupation ends. It will never again be the unitary, secular state of before, and many will be unhappy with the ethnic/sectarian flavour and political style of the particular region they end up in, but it is much too soon to conclude that everything will collapse into chaos and random violence when the Americans leave. The Iraqis, perhaps after a few false starts, might just start clearing up the mess.

On the other hand, they might not. It is possible that the civil war trundles on for a couple of years in the same style as the Lebanese civil war did, with the occasional street or village falling to the other side but no dramatic territorial changes, until the Americans finally leave, and that the Iraqis are by then too embittered and alienated by all the killing and ethnic/sectarian cleansing to put their country back together under the

2005 constitution. Let us construct a tree of branching proba-
bilities, and consider where the various branches might lead.

The Shia-majority region, including most of Baghdad, will
be ruled either by the conventional religious parties like SCIRI
and al-Dawa with the moral support of moderate ayatollahs
like Sistani, or by the much more radical Moqtada al-Sadr
(who would still only be in his mid-thirties) – or perhaps by an
alliance of the two. Kurdistan will either have retained its legal
status as a highly autonomous part of Iraq, or it will have
declared independence under the same leadership that it has
now. And the Sunni-dominated western provinces will be –
what? A breakaway state dominated by the radical Islamists
who have played a steadily growing role in the Sunni resistance
to the U.S. occupation and an exporter of terrorism to the rest
of the Arab world and beyond? A lawless region, still formally
within Iraq, that is ravaged by a new war for control between
the Islamists and the conservative tribal forces? Or just part of
Greater Syria?

The Kurds are the easiest to predict, because they will retain
their current arm's-length relationship with Arab Iraq, or if
need be just with Shia Iraq, for as long as they possibly can. The
three Kurdish provinces are the one part of Iraq where there
already is peace and even a fair measure of prosperity –
there are plenty of construction cranes in Suleymaniye, Irbil,
and Dohuk – so they have a lot to lose. The civil war down
south is unlikely to affect them much, even economically, and
their constitutional link with Baghdad gives them protection
from the threat of a Turkish invasion without imposing many
burdens in return. Indeed, the current constitutional arrange-
ment gives the Kurds more influence in Baghdad than the
capital exercises over them. The only thing that could provoke

a really serious rupture between the two would be a failure by Baghdad to act on the constitutional promise to organize a referendum to decide the fate of Kirkuk and other disputed areas claimed by the Kurds.

"We are a different nation. Kurds are not Arabs. We happen to live in a place called Iraq. Federalism gives us the right to control our areas. The time is past for the centre to control Kurdistan."

– Massoud Barzani, head of the
Kurdish Democratic Party, November 2004

There is ample scope for conflict over Kirkuk and the other areas in dispute, unfortunately, since article 140 of the constitution does not define exactly who will be entitled to vote in the referendum that will decide their future political home. The Kurdish Regional Government (KRG) rules over about 4 million Kurds in an area the size of Switzerland, but there are at least a million other Kurds living in the disputed areas – and there used to be more, since from the 1960s onwards the Ba'ath Party pursued an "Arabization" policy that forcibly expelled Kurds and other ethnic minorities from their homes and replaced them with Sunni and Shia Arab settlers brought up from the south.

Now the Kurds want their lands back. The problem is especially acute in the oil-producing region dominated by Kirkuk, Iraq's fourth-largest city, which lies just beyond the Green Line, the KRG's current border. When Saddam's regime fell in 2003, Kurdish Pesh Merga troops moved into the city, and since then substantial numbers of Kurdish refugees have returned. Many have not yet recovered their homes from the Arab settlers and are living in tents, however, and there is no agreement on how to compensate and resettle Arab families who may have been living in their present (confiscated) homes for as long as forty years. To make matters more complicated, there is also a large Turkoman minority in the city who definitely do not wish to live under Kurdish rule. Meanwhile, Arab militias have begun to establish themselves in Kirkuk, and suicide bombers have begun targeting Kurdish areas to foment civil war.

There is also an Arab–Kurdish confrontation in Mosul, a city of almost 2 million that straddles the Tigris close to the current border of Kurdistan. One-third of the city's people and most of the rural population between there and the borders of the KRG are Kurdish (according to the Kurdish authorities, though Arabs dispute this), but about seventy thousand Kurds fled Mosul in 2006 in fear of Sunni Arab death squads associated with the city's police, who are exclusively Arab. Two mainly Kurdish army divisions, under Kurdish commanders, are based very near to the city, and the Kurds believe that in a fair referendum they would get all of Mosul province east of the Tigris, including the eastern half of the city, and the districts of Sinjar and Tel Afar west of the river as well – but they don't know if they will get a fair referendum.

It is expecting a lot to ask any regime to give up territory it currently holds, whether justly or unjustly, and that is essentially what the Kurds are asking of their Shia Arab partners in government in Baghdad. It is only the extreme weakness of Iraqi Arabs at the moment that makes it even remotely possible. But the Kurdish leaders have little room to compromise, since both of the traditional political parties, the Kurdish Democratic Party (linked to the Barzani dynasty) and the Patriotic Union of Kurdistan (tied to the Talabani dynasty) are under strong pressure from a younger generation of Kurds who have grown impatient with their feudal structure and their compromising ways. The two parties managed to create a joint government for the KRG in May 2006, but they were at war with each other only thirteen years ago and until recently they ruled western and eastern Kurdistan as separate fiefdoms. Now they must contend with a more modern, democratic form of politics both at home and down in Baghdad, and they absolutely must get the Kirkuk region and its huge oil reserves, since without that they will not have the prospect of financial independence in their future. It will be tricky to make a deal that will keep everybody happy, or at least not entirely miserable.

If the Kurdish–Shia alliance in Baghdad breaks down and a new civil war pitting Kurds against Arabs and Turkomans erupts in the disputed territories, things may get much more exciting, for that could drive the Kurds into a declaration of independence from Iraq. They would have no trouble in making it stick against Baghdad, because their Pesh Merga militia, now formally incorporated into the new Iraqi army (but only formally) is easily the most powerful fighting force in the country apart from the U.S. Army. The danger is that independence would immediately expose them to the threat of attack by Turkey.

Ankara has long been adamant that it will not tolerate the emergence of an independent Kurdish state adjacent to the area of southeastern Turkey where Turkey's own large Kurdish minority lives, and where the rebel Kurdistan Worker's Party (PKK) has been waging an on-and-off guerrilla and terrorist war against the Turkish state for the past quarter-century. The PKK has at times used Iraqi Kurdistan as a safe rear area for its operations, and the Turkish army has crossed into the territory of Iraqi Kurdistan a number of times to attack the PKK's bases there. Ankara has also publicly vowed to protect the interests of the Turkomans in disputed Kirkuk – and to complicate matters still further, both Iran and Syria, which have restive Kurdish minorities of their own, also see an independent Kurdistan as a threat.

The emergence of an independent Kurdish state in the Middle East, only ninety years after it was promised to the Kurds in the Treaty of Sèvres at the end of the First World War, would make large waves throughout the region, for there are about 30 million Kurds in the area where the borders of Iran, Iraq, Syria, and Turkey converge: they are the largest ethnic group in the world without an independent state of their own. But it need not mean instant war and chaos. Despite its threats, Turkey might well be willing to acquiesce in such a change provided it got very solid guarantees that an independent Kurdistan would not encourage Kurdish separatism in Turkey or offer shelter to anti-Turkish rebels.

Turkey is a Western-oriented state that is seeking membership in the European Union, and the last thing it needs is to get sucked into a tangled Middle Eastern quarrel that would involve it in military rule over 5 million hostile Iraqi Kurds and, presumably, in a technical state of war with Iraq. The Turkish state is capable of rationality, and if it cannot frighten the Iraqi Kurds out of declaring independence it would probably settle for a deal that minimizes their ability to exercise influence over Turkish Kurds. Iran would likely be open to similar guarantees. Things could go dreadfully wrong in northern Iraq, but there is a decent chance that they won't. The same cannot be said for the rest of the country.

*"I have moved my family to a safe place. I have even made a will
and I continually move around so they have trouble knowing exactly
where I am."*

— Moqtada al-Sadr, February 2007

The United States has tried to "kill or capture" Moqtada al-Sadr
several times, and the "surge" strategy it adopted in early 2007
seemed likely to involve an attempt to take control of the
sprawling slum of Sadr City, his stronghold in eastern Baghdad,
so he was right to take precautions. But the United States has
never tried to understand what kind of phenomenon he is.

The U.S. occupation authorities had regular dealings from
the start with the Shia religious parties whose leaders came
back from exile in Iran and elsewhere after the invasion, and
also with Grand Ayatollah Ali al-Sistani, the senior Shia cleric
in Iraq (although the latter would never meet them in person).
Once the United States had given in to the Shia demand for
early elections in early 2004, they were all on the same side, at
least until the Shias actually had political power at last and
could order the Americans to leave.

The United States made continual attempts to dilute and
undermine Shia political power because it was deeply uneasy
about the close relations between the leaders in Iraq and their
counterparts in Iran, but once it had made its commitment it
basically stuck to it. Iyad Allawi, Ibrahim al-Jaafari, Nouri al-
Maliki, all the prime ministers, elected or unelected, whom it
has approved since the invasion of 2003 were sophisticated men
in suits, Shias who were also acceptable to the "mainstream"
Shia secular and religious authorities. Whereas Moqtada al-
Sadr is a bearded young cleric in dark robes and a turban
whose disturbing eyes follow you from a thousand posters on

the walls of Baghdad, and the U.S. authorities never had any time for him at all.

That is strange in a way, because he is certainly not pro-Iranian: they are deeply suspicious of him, and he of them. On the other hand, he is a genuine Iraqi and Arab nationalist, which is a bit of a problem if you are an occupying power in an Arab country – and his anti-Americanism is deep and hereditary: his father would often begin his sermons with "No, no to America; no, no to Israel; no, no to the Devil." And he has the largest, most devoted following of anybody in the country. They would literally die for him. Thousands already have.

Moqtada al-Sadr is practically the last of his line. His uncle, Mohammed Baqr al-Sadr, formed the "Sadrist" movement in the 1950s in an attempt to bring Shia Islam closer to the people. The traditional Shia religious authorities, the Hawza, wanted nothing to do with politics, whereas he wanted to combat the influence of the Baathist and Iraqi Communist parties, both stridently secular and revolutionary, that were fighting it out for the loyalty of the masses. Baqr felt that far too many young Shias, especially working-class Shias, were falling for these alien ideologies and neglecting their faith, so he concluded that Shia religious leaders must become more politically engaged. The Baathists (mostly Sunni) eventually won in the late 1960s, and carried out one of the largest massacres of Communists (mostly Shia) seen in any Muslim country except Indonesia. The Shias were losers and victims yet again, and young, radical working-class Shias had nowhere to turn. Al-Sadr became a very influential figure among the Shia masses, even though he never became an ayatollah.

Saddam Hussein, who had assumed absolute control of the Ba'ath Party in 1979, became alarmed at the rise in Shia fervour in Iraq after the revolution in Iran that year that overthrew the Shah and put Ayatollah Khomeini in power. In 1980, therefore, he had Mohammed Baqr al-Sadr, his sister, and hundreds of his supporters murdered, but the movement did not die, and when living standards for working-class Shias began to collapse under the impact of sanctions after the Gulf War of 1991, they found a new leader.

More precisely, Saddam found him, for religious belief was on the rise in Iraq in response to the failure of the secular regimes, as it was in all the Arab countries, and the once entirely secular dictator needed to co-opt someone who could deflect the anger of the Shia masses, already poor and rapidly getting poorer. What made him think that the brother of the al-Sadr he had killed was the right man for the job is beyond understanding, but at the beginning of the 1990s, Saddam chose Mohammed Sadiq al-Sadr, Moqtada's father, for this role.

Sadiq seized the opportunity, and some of what he said suited Saddam's purposes: he was an Iraqi patriot, he called for unity between Sunnis and Shias, and he condemned any foreign interference, American or Iranian, in Iraq's affairs. But he also condemned Saddam's tyranny, knowing full well that it would eventually lead to his own death. In 1999, Saddam's security men ambushed Sadiq and two of his sons in their car in the Shia holy city of Najaf and killed them. Only Moqtada survived, and they didn't bother with him because he seemed harmless. Then, four years later, the American army arrived in Baghdad and Saddam was gone.

The savage looting that swept Baghdad after the fall of Saddam was a measure of how angry and alienated working-class Shias were: totally impoverished, jobless, and alternately patronized and neglected by the Shia political and religious establishment. They didn't trust the religious hierarchy in Najaf, they didn't trust the exiles coming back to rebuild the Shia religious parties, and they certainly didn't trust the Americans. Neither did Moqtada, so he was their man, and within days he was leading a mass pilgrimage of hundreds of thousands of men walking to Karbala, something that had been banned under Saddam for many years. Within weeks, his picture was on walls all over the poorer Shia neighbourhoods of Baghdad, often flanked by those of his martyred father and uncle. Within months, he was probably the most powerful Shia leader in the country.

It's not really about religion; it's about class. Iraq is a highly urbanized country where the social gulf between the middle class and the urban poor, whether Shia or Sunni, is positively Victorian. But more of the Shias are poor, and without prior fame, without wealth, without being a particularly articulate speaker, just on the basis of his heritage and his willingness to express plainly what they felt, Moqtada al-Sadr became their leader and their idol. By the end of 2003, he already had the biggest militia in Iraq, the Mahdi Army (and until recently, its volunteers were not only unpaid but had to buy their own weapons). By April 2004, when the Americans closed down his movement's newspaper and ordered his arrest, he was ready to take them on in open battle.

He lost, of course, and hundreds or even thousands of his untrained fighters died in gun battles where the American kill ratio was probably one hundred-to-one. But Moqtada survived because the mainstream Shia authorities persuaded the occupation authorities that killing him might trigger a general uprising, and he walked away from the fight with a moral victory. The Mahdi Army fought another round with the

Americans in August 2004, but after that Moqtada learned his lesson and stopped getting his people killed for nothing. He backed candidates in the 2005 elections despite publicly declaring a boycott of it, and ended up with thirty-two supporters in the National Assembly, which gave him the balance of power in the tortuous negotiations to form a government. As a result, his movement ended up with six cabinet seats and huge leverage on Prime Minister al-Maliki.

While other Shias, notably the SCIRI-controlled Interior Ministry police, began responding to the suicide-bomb attacks in the crowded streets and markets of the poorest Shia districts in Baghdad with targeted and random killings of Sunnis as early as mid-2004, Moqtada al-Sadr's Mahdi Army was not involved in such murders until the bombing of the Askariya shrine in February 2006, and even then there is no evidence that he approved of such killings. He continues to deny any involvement by his followers in the grisly sectarian killings that are now such a large part of daily life in Iraq, and he really may not be in full control of all the people now claiming to be part of the Mahdi Army. He has never made a sectarian speech, and is trying very hard to avoid being drawn into battle with the Americans in Sadr City, preferring to stay alive and wait them out – for in a couple of years, he could effectively be the leader of Iraq.

We can easily guess what any future Iraqi government led by conventional Shia leaders drawn from Dawa and SCIRI and closely associated with the senior Shia clergy would look like, for we have seen several such governments already. They would remain under the thumb of the United States for the time being, of course, but they would probably not behave in drastically different ways once they were free of American supervision.

They would naturally seek to consolidate Shia political supremacy in Arab Iraq, but that task is largely complete already. They would work to revive the Iraqi economy, beginning with the badly damaged oil industry, because their political clientele depends on that economy for its well-being. They would try to diminish the intense sectarianism engendered by the occupation, because that makes governing the society more difficult. And they would be open to deals that share the wealth and even some political power at least with Kurds (they have made such deals already), and very probably with Sunni Arabs as well (since the alternatives are to wage an eternal civil war or to see the country's borders change). They might not succeed in all these policies, but those would be their priorities.

They would be closer to Iran than any Arab country has been in centuries, for Iran is the one really powerful Shia country. It is also Iraq's biggest and most important neighbour, and many of the leaders in the mainstream Shia political parties have spent large parts of their adult lives in exile in Iran. But that does not necessarily or even probably mean that they would be eager volunteers in any political adventures that Iran might have in mind in the Arab world, such as inciting Shias to revolt in Saudi Arabia, Bahrain, or Lebanon. (Not to say that that is what Iran will do, but you know how people worry.) Their Arab and Iraqi identities may be a bit compromised by their strong Iranian links, but the mainstream Shia leaders would have a country to run if they stay in power. It is a country whose economy has been going backwards for almost thirty years, and it will not be possible to repair it if they emulate Saddam Hussein and pick quarrels with all their neighbours.

The real question is not what the conventional Shia politicians would do, but what would happen if they lose power to the untutored rabble-rouser, the representative of the despised and the downtrodden, Moqtada al-Sadr. He would certainly be worse at holding a federal Iraq together, because his intense religiosity frightens the Kurds, his clear and visible identification with the Shia tradition frightens the Sunni Arabs, and his alliance with the poor even frightens middle-class Shia Arabs. But would he join Iran in some joint Shia offensive to destabilize neighbouring Arab regimes and incite Shia uprisings in the few other Arab countries with substantial Shia minorities? Improbable.

Moqtada al-Sadr is as much an Iraqi nationalist as he is a Shia leader. In fact, a big part of his appeal to the Shia masses is that, unlike his more sophisticated rivals in other parts of the Shia political spectrum, he is an open and unashamed Iraqi patriot. The likelihood that he would unthinkingly do Iran's bidding is too small to calculate. His views on most existing Arab regimes are not known, but they are probably not complimentary. On the other hand, the mere fact that they are not known suggests that meddling in other Arab countries will not be his highest priority. His political mandate, if he gained supreme power, would be to lift the poorest section of Iraqi society (most of which happens to be Shia) out of its current desperate plight, but he has never taken a sectarian line on any public issue.

None of the above guarantees that Moqtada al-Sadr, or indeed some other Shia politician we haven't even heard of yet, will not turn Iraq into hell for its citizens and a threat to all its neighbours. After all, Saddam Hussein did that for a while, and nobody saw him coming. But the fact that Iraqi politics now includes a substantial democratic component backed by a free press means that it is rather less likely to happen. Bringing democracy to Iraq was not the primary purpose of the American invasion, and there are easier ways of getting to democracy that do not involve perhaps half a million dead and six years of foreign military occupation. But the fact is that Iraq now has a more or less democratic system despite the civil war, the endemic corruption, and all the rest, and it has a fighting chance of keeping it. Under almost any permutation of possible political outcomes, it is extremely unlikely to allow U.S. military bases of any sort to remain (except perhaps in Iraqi Kurdistan, where the authority of the government in Baghdad will probably remain very weak).

So two regions down and one to go, and still no apocalypse in sight. What about the Sunni Arabs of Iraq? Well, consider how they felt as they watched the televised scene of Saddam Hussein's execution on December 30, 2006. According to the Sunni calendar (but not the Shia) it was the first day of Eid, the great Islamic feast that has a similar social and emotional content to Christmas in the Christian tradition, and they would have been aware that the choice of that date to kill the former leader was probably not an accident. Not many of them would have felt much sympathy for Saddam as a person, but they would have been intensely aware that in some symbolic ways he was standing there as a symbol of Sunni defeat. Then as Saddam launches into his final profession of faith, with the noose already around his neck, the witnesses around the gallows, obviously Shias, begin to shout at him.

"Moqtada, Moqtada, Moqtada," one chants. Saddam repeats the name dismissively, then smiles and says: "Do you consider this bravery?" Another voice shouts: "Go to hell!" Saddam, accusing his enemies of destroying the country he once led, replies: "The hell that is Iraq?" Another Shia shouts, "Long live Mohammed Baqr al-Sadr," but Saddam begins his prayer once again: "I profess that there is no God but God and that Muhammad. . . ." The executioner pulls the lever without waiting for him to finish, and Saddam plunges through the trap door to his death.

The Shias had every right to hate Saddam, but the symbolic message was pretty frightening for any Sunni Arab in Iraq. The whole community is bewildered and terrified by its sudden drop in status, and that has made it much more receptive to extremist ideas.

In the first year of the Sunni Arab resistance to the U.S. occupation, the typical local commander would have been a whisky-drinking ex-army officer and Ba'ath Party member who wore his religion lightly, if at all. In the fifth year of the resistance, he is more likely to be a devout and austere man of relatively humble background who thinks that killing Americans is a sacred duty, not just a necessary job, and who also thinks that barbers who shave people's beards and give un-Islamic haircuts should be killed. The latter man poses a considerably greater problem for Iraq and for its neighbours.

The ideological slide from nationalist resistance movement to Islamist jihad had some help from outside (all the freelance fanatics from Saudi Arabia and elsewhere who showed up to help the cause by blowing themselves up in public places), but it was mostly due to an internal dynamic familiar from other societies under foreign military occupation: when the struggle becomes all-encompassing, the absolutists tend to drive out the relativists, and the ideology becomes extreme and rigid. The dominant elements in the Sunni resistance today subscribe to very intolerant variants of Islam such as Salafism, which treats all non-Salafist Muslims as little better than infidels and preaches universal revolution to cleanse Islam of impure practices. If they ultimately prevail in the western provinces of Iraq, they will make very awkward neighbours.

The civil war, of course, gives them additional power and authority, especially in mixed urban areas, since they are the people that threatened Sunni neighbourhoods and communities turn to first for protection. And while many sophisticated Baghdadi Sunnis see them as a necessary evil, to the west and north, in tough, smaller cities like Ramadi, Fallujah, and Tikrit, they fit right in with the local values. So will the western, Sunni region of Iraq end up as an enclave of extremists and a source of ideological infection for the Arab states next door?

The problem the Sunnis faced when the Americans invaded was that the other two major groups in Iraq had two militias each – KDP and PUK for the Kurds, together known as Pesh Merga, and the Badr Brigade and the Mahdi Army for the Shias – but they had none. They hadn't needed one, because the Sunnis basically ran everything, and the army, the police, and the secret police all belonged to them. But suddenly all those organizations were gone, and all they had left were the various resistance groups that formed more or less spontaneously (although there may have been a Baathist plan of sorts for post-war resistance). If you had administered a test for religiosity to the various Iraqi communities a year before the invasion, the Sunnis would have fallen about midway between the very devout Shias and the largely secular Kurds, but those many different Sunni resistance groups evolved in the predictable way, and within a year or two the Sunnis found themselves in thrall to the Salafist extremists who dominated the resistance.

Nobody knows whether this abnormal situation will survive

the occupation and civil war that brought it into being. If the more secular and less militant forces in Sunni Arab society, from ex-Baathists to traditional tribal leaders, manage to reassert their leading roles once the Americans leave and the civil war ends (two separate events, though perhaps closely linked), then neither Iraq nor its neighbours will have a huge problem on their hands. The Sunni Arabs will grudgingly make the deals that allow them to take up a diminished but still satisfactory role in Iraqi society, and the neighbours will breathe a long sigh of relief. But if the Sunni Arab majority areas of Iraq turn into Taliban West and start trying to export radical Islamist revolution to the region, then everybody is in for a very rough ride.

My guess is that they will opt for a quiet life and manage to make it stick, even though that would probably require shooting a few of the former heroes of the resistance (as so often happens at the end of guerrilla wars). But we must consider the alternative: that the Islamists take power in the Sunni Arab region, and start trying to spread their revolutionary doctrine throughout the Arab world. They would have little luck within the rest of Iraq, where the Shias are automatically inoculated against Sunni extremism and the Kurds are resolutely secular, but there are more vulnerable countries across the border. The three within easiest reach are Syria, ruled with an iron hand for forty years by a family dynasty drawn from the country's Alawi (Shia) minority; Jordan, where the monarch's family originally hails from Arabia but two-thirds of the population is Palestinian; and Saudi Arabia itself, where there is already a Salafist revolutionary movement that regularly carries out terrorist attacks (although it has been relatively quiet since a large number of arrests in 2004–5). No wonder Saudi Arabia has ordered the urgent construction of a double fence barring the entire 900-kilometre (550-mile) length of its border with Iraq. It will include buried movement sensors, ultraviolet night-vision cameras, face-recognition software, and quite probably automated weapons in addition to the usual electrified chain-link, concertina wire, dry moats, mines, and command posts and it will cost an estimated $8.5 billion, but price is not an issue when the very survival of the regime may be at stake.

Fences don't stop ideas, however, and the main threat to all of these regimes is that they suffer from a serious lack of credibility with their own people. Only Jordan has anything resembling democratic institutions, and only Syria has kept its Arab nationalist credentials spotless by avoiding a close relationship with the United States. The regimes are all vulnerable to Islamist revolutions, and they know it.

One option for dealing with the threat, if the post-occupation Iraqi government cannot or will not bring the western provinces to heel, is good, old-fashioned military force: invade western Iraq and crush the source of the infection. That is what the United States did when it invaded Afghanistan, and what it said it was doing when it invaded Iraq, so it must be an option available to Iraq's neighbours, too. The Iraqi army in its current state certainly couldn't stop them. On the other hand, there is no reason to think that other Arab countries would have an easier time occupying part of Iraq than the United States did, and there is the awkward question of what you do with western Iraq next, once the extremists have all gone to ground. Do you just hand it back to the government in Baghdad that couldn't control it in the first place? Do you occupy it permanently (but it stretches all the way to the western suburbs of Baghdad, where there are 2 million Sunnis)? Do you detach it from Iraq entirely and bundle it into Syria, where the main opposition to the Baathist dictatorship is also Sunni extremists? Damascus wouldn't be keen on that.

There is no military solution to the problem (which is not to say that it won't be attempted). The upheavals in Iraq only emphasize the dangers that regimes in neighbouring countries already face from homegrown Islamist revolutionaries, and the solution is to start changing their own political systems in ways that defuse the discontent. If they cannot do that (and some of them probably cannot), then they are fair game for revolution whether western Iraq goes Islamist or not. Revolutions are never really exported from one country to another, but sometimes the seeds of revolution fall on fertile ground. The trick, if a regime wants to survive, is to get other seeds into that ground first.

As for the "terrorist threat," the fear that a breakaway "Sunni triangle" of western Iraq under Islamist control would become a terrorist breeding ground may be a bit overdone. Western Iraq is serving that function now, to some extent, because the resistance to the occupation hones both the skills and the ideology of radical Islamists from Iraq and abroad, but the whole notion of "breeding grounds" and "terrorist bases" is a misconception based on analogies from conventional military operations. You don't need a whole country to be a terrorist; a couple of rooms will do.

CHAPTER V

THE TERRORIST BANDWAGON

"We've got to win this war on terror . . . and it's going to be fought overseas, or if we don't win there, it's going to be fought here in the United States."

– Sen. Bill Frist (Senate Majority Leader at the time),
September 2006

It's true. Every terrorist shot dead while attacking a convoy on the Baghdad Airport Highway is one less terrorist attacking commuters on the approach roads to New York's Holland Tunnel. If American troops weren't in Iraq, people in New Jersey would never be able to make it to Manhattan, and there would be a mujahid with a rocket-propelled grenade on every overpass in America.

No? That's not what Senator Frist meant? Well, what did he mean? How does fighting terrorists in Iraq and Afghanistan prevent some other terrorists getting on a plane in Saudi Arabia or Pakistan – or more likely Germany or Spain – and flying to the United States? Are we even talking about the same people?

The average Taliban fighter would stand out a bit in the immigration queue at the airport, whereas some evildoer who speaks English and has a good forged passport saying that she's Dutch might slip through without attracting too much notice. How does "fighting this battle overseas" stop her? It would make some sense if we were talking about Hitler's legions or the Imperial Japanese Navy ("If we don't stop them at Midway, we'll be fighting them off the California coast!"), but how does it apply to airline passengers with box-cutters?

It is a huge mistake to look at the "Global War on Terror" (or the Global War on Islam, as it is known in some circles) as a conventional military operation in which you have to hold the line against the enemy. It is probably literally true that not one of the tens of thousands of people that the U.S. armed forces have killed overseas in the past five years would ever have shown up in the United States if they had been left alive. *Different* people might have shown up with the intention to do the United States harm, but the U.S. Army would never even have caught a glimpse of them.

The war on terror is a bandwagon, however, and everybody has climbed on board. Especially the Pentagon, which in early 2006 officially adopted the concept of the "Long War." "The struggle . . . may well be fought in dozens of other countries simultaneously and for many years to come," said the four-yearly strategy review submitted to Congress in February 2006 – and thereupon the Pentagon proceeded to ask for $513 billion for defence spending in 2007.

Pretty cheeky, when the sharp end of the threat is more likely to be civilians with high explosives, as in the attacks in London in July 2005, but General Peter Pace, chairman of the U.S. joint chiefs of staff, explained earnestly that "we face a ruthless enemy intent on destroying our way of life and an uncertain future." A "ruthless enemy"? Yes. "Intent on destroying our way of life"? No, they just want you out of the Middle East. What do they care about how Americans live their lives? "An uncertain future"? Well, yes, but when wasn't the future uncertain? And very little of the uncertainty right now is due to terrorism: worry about global climate change, the rise of China, or bird 'flu if you have the time. So how is terrorism going to change the future of the United States?

The U.S. armed forces have found the most plausible justification for military spending since the end of the late, lamented Cold War, and they are playing it for all they are worth. There is a good deal of cynicism in this, because in their own staff colleges they teach their officers that terrorism is primarily a domestic security problem, best addressed by police surveillance, intelligence-gathering, and barriers to free movement like airport security checks. Terrorists are civilians, and they are usually to be found in places where the uniformed military are absent. But if the public wants a "war" on terror, they'll be happy to provide one. Just give them the budget, and they'll fight it.

To the man who has only a hammer, everything looks like a nail. The United States has very large conventional armed forces that are continually looking for ways to make themselves useful, and relatively few people skilled in the subtle, low-profile intelligence tasks most relevant in countering a terrorist threat, so the temptation to turn a "war on terror" into a conventional military operation is overwhelming. That is why President Bush got away for so long with his constantly repeated assertion that "the safety of America depends on the outcome of the battle in the streets of Baghdad." It is patent nonsense, of course, but it sounds a lot more sensible to the average American than "the safety of America depends on foreign policies that do not inspire rage and hatred in very large numbers of people elsewhere, and relentless, detailed intelligence gathering to thwart those who plan terrorist attacks against us." The conventional thinking in the United States tends not only to militarize any conflict in which the United States is involved, it actually tries to force every conflict into the mould of the last great war in which the United States won a decisive military victory: the Second World War. There is always a global plan by evil people to take over the world, and the way to defeat it is always with American military power.

That is what happened with Vietnam forty years ago. In the 1960s, the United States talked itself into believing that the Communist insurgents in Vietnam were not local anticolonial revolutionaries but the spearhead of an international Communist conspiracy to take over the world, with the Chinese Communists backing them and the Soviet Union behind China. If Vietnam fell to the Commies, then like dominoes Cambodia, Thailand, Malaysia, and the Philippines would follow. If we didn't stop them now in Vietnam, we would soon be fighting them on the beaches of California. President Lyndon B. Johnson declared that Americans were "watchmen on the walls of world freedom" and sent more than half a million young Americans to fight in the hills and paddies of South Vietnam. More than 2.5 million American soldiers served in Vietnam between 1963 and 1973, and fifty-eight thousand of them were killed there during those years, together with about 3 million Vietnamese, but in the end the local Communists won, reunited the country – and stopped fighting.

Cambodia fell to local Communists too, but only because Henry Kissinger, then Richard Nixon's secretary of state, had destabilized it by backing a military coup against the Cambodian king who had successfully kept his country out of the fighting in the former French Indochina for many years. Thailand didn't fall, Malaysia didn't fall, the Philippines didn't fall, and the Communists never reached California. It should already have been clear to Washington that the Soviet Union and China saw each other as enemies, but somehow that got overlooked. It should have been clear that China and Vietnam weren't the best of friends either – within a few more years they were at war with each other – but that was overlooked, too. There was no world conspiracy, and the Vietnam War was a post-colonial, nationalist war that had little significance even for the U.S.–Soviet Cold War, but the paradigm overwhelmed the reality. All the deaths were wasted.

Now the relatively minor threat of Islamist terrorism is being forced into the same mould. It is the "Global War on Terror" or "The Long War," and it is going to be fought all over the world, with armies and air forces, for years and years. In a major foreign policy speech to the National Endowment for Democracy in October 2005, President Bush offered an expanded version of why he believes that Iraq is now the "central front" in the "global war on terror," and therefore a battle in which the United States must "prevail." Iraq is now the prime target for "militant networks," he explained, and "the militants believe that controlling one country will rally the Muslim masses, enabling them to overthrow all moderate governments in the region, and establish a radical Islamic empire that spans from Spain to Indonesia." Then, with the resources of this world-spanning empire at their disposal, they would "advance their stated agenda: to develop weapons of mass destruction, to destroy Israel, to intimidate Europe, to assault the American people and to blackmail our government into isolation." (I wouldn't be surprised if they tried to steal our vital organs and sell them for spare parts, too.)

It is a faithfully reproduced working model of the Vietnam era's "domino theory": if "the militants" win in Iraq, then eventually they'll conquer the world. Except that while Lyndon Johnson clearly believed in the domino theory right down to his boot soles, it's not clear that President Bush really believes what he says in the same guileless way. Listen to the way he uses the words: "the militants believe." He never says that *he* believes that "the militants" are going to move on from Iraq to establish a world-spanning Islamic empire from Spain to Indonesia, because that is simply ridiculous. *They* may believe it, but then they also believe that they will enjoy the services of seventy-two virgins after they are martyred for the cause. Does George W. Bush believe it? One wonders.

So how might we get a realistic measure of the scale and nature of the terrorist threat? One way would be simply to ignore the rhetoric and pay some attention to the statistics. Another would be to analyze the terrorists' strategy – for they do have strategies; being wicked does not make you stupid – and figure out what it is that they hope to achieve.

The statistics, helpfully provided by the U.S. State Department, are quite comforting. The worst years for international terrorism – defined as "the targeting of non-combatants or property by non-state agents" – were actually in the mid-1980s, in 1985–88, when the most spectacular attacks were on airlines. One hundred and eighty-nine Americans died in the Libyan bombing of Pan-Am 103 over Lockerbie, Scotland, in 1988, and 329 people died in the bombing, presumably by Sikh terrorists, of Air-India 182 in 1985. Canada lost 285 citizens in the latter attack, proportionally as many as the United States did on 9/11. After that, however, the phenomenon went into steady decline. There were upward blips on the graph in 1991 and 1998, and there was another, smaller blip in 2001, but after that the fall in the annual number of casualties resumed. In the three years after 2001, which include the Bali and Madrid attacks, deaths from international terrorism were down to one-third of the level that prevailed in the 1980s. (Since 2004, the number of attacks recorded by the State Department has risen sharply again, but this is in large measure because it takes account of the rapidly growing number of attacks by "al-Qaeda in Mesopotamia," which most people would not consider to be international terrorism.)

This picture of a declining threat from international terrorism is counterintuitive, but that is because our impression of the scale of the terrorist problem is shaped mainly by the mass media, and the amount of coverage devoted to terrorism fluctuates quite independently of the actual numbers. The previous peak in media coverage was in 1986, when President Ronald Reagan ordered the bombing of Libya for supporting terrorism, but globally the number of attacks and deaths was higher the following year – and media coverage fell by three-quarters because the U.S. armed forces were not involved. Conversely, media coverage of terrorism has been consistently at record highs since 2001, although actual deaths from terrorist attacks were at record lows until the invasion of Iraq.

"If we were not fighting and destroying this enemy in Iraq, they would not be idle. They would be plotting and killing Americans across the world and within our own borders. By fighting these terrorists in Iraq, Americans in uniform are defeating a direct threat to the American people."

– President George W. Bush, November 30, 2005

Media coverage is essentially driven by how interested politicians are in an issue, since it is political rhetoric that sets the news agenda most of the time. Actual terrorist events only occur sporadically, so if the politicians aren't talking about terrorism then there is usually nothing to report on the matter. It is the American media, above all, that set the international news agenda, and since 9/11 American politicians have been in overdrive on the subject. President Bush, in particular, has chosen to make the "war on terror" the defining theme of his presidency and talks about it at every possible opportunity, so coverage of terrorism has gone through the roof.

So much for the statistics; what about the Islamists' strategy? It was the classic terrorist strategy: trick your far more powerful opponent into doing things that will ultimately serve your own political purposes. Get the Americans to invade Muslim countries, and that will alienate and radicalize Muslims and turn them against their pro-American governments, which will then be overthrown – and the Islamists themselves will come to power.

It was actually identical to the Irish Republican Army's strategy in Northern Ireland in 1967–2000, except that bin Laden was operating on a transcontinental scale. The IRA began by luring the British government into committing troops to the province to deal with the terrorism, then provoked the army into severely repressive measures that drove the (Catholic) population into the IRA's arms, and finally waged a long guerrilla struggle that was intended to wear down the British government's will to go on defending the existing political order in Northern Ireland. If you were writing the *Terrorism for Dummies* handbook, this would be Strategy 1A.

The IRA didn't win, at least in the short run, because Catholics still comprise only a minority of Northern Ireland's population and the British government didn't give up and go home. But Osama bin Laden doesn't face that handicap – the vast majority of people in the Arab world are Muslims – and his strategy is making some progress. Not that it is really just his any more: as he said shortly after escaping from the Tora Bora caves in late 2001: "If Osama lives or dies does not matter. . . . The awakening has started." And it has, in the sense that the model bin Laden constructed in al-Qaeda is proliferating across the Arab world. Abu Musab al-Zarqawi's group of Islamist terrorists in Iraq sought and received permission to start calling themselves "Al-Qaeda in Mesopotamia," although none of its leading figures has ever met bin Laden. More recently, an Algerian terrorist organization left over from the ghastly civil war of the 1990s, called the Salafist Group for Preaching and Combat, received "official recognition" from Ayman al-Zawahiri, bin Laden's deputy, and changed its name to "Al-Qaeda in the Maghreb." (Al-Qaeda franchises always use geographical terms rather than country names, since the ideology condemns the very existences of separate states within the Muslim world.)

But it is only the name that is being franchised, and in most cases not even that. What bin Laden has done is to articulate an ideology and a strategy, demonstrate their usefulness, and set them loose in the world for Muslims anywhere to adopt and adapt as they wish. Al-Qaeda in its original form barely exists any more, but it doesn't need to. As U.S. general Michael Hayden, then deputy director of national intelligence, said in April 2006: "New jihadist networks and cells, sometimes united by little more than their anti-western agenda, are increasingly likely to emerge. If this trend continues, threats to the U.S. at home and abroad will become more diverse and that could lead to increasing attacks worldwide."

The two most important (but widely misunderstood) facts about "Islamist terrorism" is that it is mainly an Arab phenomenon, although it always claims to act on behalf of Muslims everywhere, and that it is a revolutionary movement whose primary goal is to overthrow Arab governments. A large majority of its adherents have always been Arabs, although they account for only about a quarter of the Muslim world's

1.3 billion people, and most of the rest are Pakistanis. (The relatively large involvement of Pakistanis stems from Partition in 1947, since when Pakistani identity has been defined almost exclusively in religious terms – and the endless dispute with India over divided Kashmir has served to radicalize young Pakistanis generation after generation.) Revolutionary Islamism is the most marginal of fringe movements in democratic Muslim countries like Turkey, Bangladesh, Malaysia, or Indonesia that have relatively successful economies. It is exclusively Sunni in its membership, and has no connection at all with Shia Iran.

Islamism is mostly an Arab phenomenon because the Arab world is a political, economic, and social disaster area. It regained its independence in the 1940s and 1950s after half a century or more of European colonial rule (having previously spent centuries under Turkish rule), but it proved to be almost uniquely unsuccessful in building modern, prosperous, and just societies. Only the African ex-colonies have done worse. Half of Arab women are illiterate. Living standards in the countries that don't have oil have been falling for decades, as vigorous population growth outstrips feeble economic growth. (Even some of the oil-rich countries are similarly affected: Saudi Arabia's per capita income fell by more than half between the mid-1980s and 2005.) There is little industry, less science, and almost no innovation. Practically all the governments of the Arab states are absolute monarchies, one-party states, or thinly disguised military dictatorships. Moreover, many of them are in practice Western dependencies, protected and in some cases subsidized by the United States because they do America's bidding.

In order to account for this extraordinary full-spectrum

failure, we need not engage in airy speculation about the alleged shortcomings of Arab culture, society, or mentality, as two obvious reasons stare us in the face. One is the corrosive effect of oil wealth on the societies that have come to depend on it, and the constant foreign meddling in their affairs that came with the oil. During the Cold War, Arab governments were routinely supported in their repressive ways by both superpowers because it was strategically important to keep them on the right side, and the habit has not died although the strategic realities have changed drastically.

The second reason is Israel. At the very moment when they achieved independence, Egypt and the countries of the Fertile Crescent were confronted with what they saw as a new Western colony in their midst, and their badly trained and poorly led post-colonial armies were ignominiously defeated by the new Israeli state in the first Arab–Israeli war of 1948–49. Palestinian refugees, in many cases deliberately driven out by the Israelis in order to ensure a large Jewish majority in the new state, flooded into the camps that sprang up around it, and Israel became a national obsession that no Arab government could ignore. There have been five more wars since then, and Israel has won them all, in most cases with highly visible American support. (The last was in Lebanon in the summer of 2006, although there is some debate, both in Israel and elsewhere, about whether it really won that one.)

Yet despite this unbroken record of failure, there has been no change of regime anywhere in the Arab world for more than forty years apart from the American overthrow of Saddam Hussein in 2003. Changes of the guard, certainly, because mortality happens. A quarter-century ago, for example, the ex-military officer who currently rules Egypt, President Hosni

Mubarak, succeeded the previous military officer who ruled the country, Anwar Sadat, who was assassinated in one of the first Islamist attacks. In 2000, Bashar al-Assad succeeded his father, Hafez al-Assad, an air force general who seized power in 1970, as president of Syria. Two years later, the young man now known as King Abdullah II of Jordan succeeded his father, Hussein, the "plucky little king," who had ruled the kingdom for forty-seven years (although everybody had expected the throne to go to Hussein's brother, Hassan, until a deathbed change of mind by Hussein). But real change? It doesn't happen in the Arab world.

So the region is filled with rage and despair. Not the broader Muslim world, where in most places the economy is growing, the government is democratic or at least edging in that direction, and people feel that they have a future. Just quite specifically the Arab world. So there are, unsurprisingly, revolutionary movements almost everywhere in the Arab world, and they command the loyalty of some of the most intelligent and industrious people in those societies. More surprisingly, the great majority of these revolutionary movements have, in this generation, an Islamist ideology.

There is a simplistic view, much too widespread in the West, that the religious fanaticism and systematic terrorism of the Islamist revolutionaries is the expression of something inherent in Islam. (My grandmother, who had an equally simple view of the world, used to tell me that "the Germans have war in their blood.") But fanaticism is generally a response of groups or societies that are under great stress, and that description would certainly fit the Arab world. Back in the 1950s and 1960s it was a fairly relaxed place where most educated people were either fashionably secular or attended Friday prayers out of long habit, and the most popular brand of politics was not Islamist but socialist – Marxist, in fact, though without the atheism that European Marxists insisted on. Even today most of the secular republics of the Arab world – Egypt, Syria, Libya, Tunisia, Algeria, and, until recently, Iraq – have their roots in revolutionary Marxism. The problem is that they failed to deliver the goods, either on development or on Palestine, and so by the 1970s they were regarded by most politically conscious people in the Arab world as worn out and overdue for replacement. Yet thirty years later, they are still there.

With the discrediting of Marxist socialism, the search was on for a new ideology, especially among the new generation of revolutionaries who wanted to overthrow all the failed existing Arab regimes. Maybe precisely because Marxism was so strenuously secular, the candidate that came out in front was Islamism. It was an old ideology dressed up in new clothes (it had last been in vogue before the First World War, when it was called pan-Islamism), but it fitted the demands of the moment very well. It built on a Sunni doctrine called Salafism, an intensely romantic vision of a single Muslim superstate ruled by sharia law that eliminated all national and class distinctions among believers and had the power to make the rest of the world respect it. (In some extreme versions, it would ultimately convert the whole world to Islam.)

The original Salafists believed that their vision could only be achieved if all the world's Muslims returned to the pure Islamic values of the first generations after the Prophet himself. The new converts to the doctrine turned that condition into a prescription: what we have to do is *make* everybody live as the first Muslims did. Then the vision will actually be realized, and Muslims (well, Arabs, really, but if you are a Salafist you have to talk in terms of all Muslims) will be rich and powerful, feared and respected once again. This is magical thinking, of course, but desperate people are often in need of magic, and there were quite a few people who were in despair about the state of the Arab world.

In the course of the 1970s, Salafism was turned into a doctrine for political revolution all across the Arab world. In the stripped-down version for public consumption, the argument went as follows: we Muslims have been losing every battle on every front for the past several centuries, and we are now poor, despised and oppressed by the West. Why has God allowed this disaster to befall His people? It is because we have turned away from Him. When we were faced with the onslaught from the West, instead of clinging to our own values and institutions, we began to copy theirs, trying to beat the West at its own game. It didn't work, and worse, as we became more and more Westernized, God turned His face away from us.

The solution to all our problems is to start living as true Muslims should. Then we will enjoy God's support once more, we will unite the whole umma (the community of the faithful all over the world), and we will start to win. In order to bring everybody back to the right ways of living their faith, however, we must first gain power in the various separate Muslim countries and use the power of the state to *force* all the fallen-away, half-Westernized Muslims back into the paths of true observance. (Here comes the revolutionary bit.) Only when we have overthrown the corrupt governments that oppress Muslims now and serve the interests of the "Zionist-Crusader alliance" will all this become possible, so our first task is revolution.

The "Zionist-Crusader alliance" is propaganda-speak for the group of countries that causes most trouble for the Arabs, and it doesn't have much resonance in the south and southeast Asian countries where most Muslims live (for Pakistani Islamists, the main enemy is Hinduism and India). There is a contradiction between the fact that revolutionary Islamism in the Arab lands is really an Arab nationalist ideology that promises to solve Arab problems, and the theoretical doctrine that denies all distinctions between Muslims and actively condemns the nationalisms that divide them. But agile minds have bridged the gap by insisting that the Arabs are the first and primary target of a Western onslaught against the whole Muslim world, so in concentrating on overthrowing the corrupt, secular governments of the Arab world – including deeply conservative and religious regimes that do not follow the Islamist path, like that of Saudi Arabia – the Islamists are in effect fighting the battles of the whole Muslim world.

For almost thirty years now, therefore, the Islamists/Salafists of the Arab world have been trying to overthrow the regimes of the Arab world and take their place, so that they can begin to apply their program for reforming Muslim society and making it truly Islamic (according to their version of true Islam). If they ever got their way with a major Arab country, it would probably look quite a lot like Afghanistan under the Taliban, for the Taliban shared the same ideas about the need to cleanse Islamic society of all corrupting Western influences and revert to some idealized version of primitive Islam. And that may explain why the Islamists have never managed to pull off a successful revolution in an Arab country in all this time.

Afghanistan has never been at the bleeding edge of social change in the Muslim world, and most Afghans were hardly Westernized at all, but even there many people chafed at the Taliban's obsession with nitpicking rules, ruthlessly enforced, about minor details of dress and behaviour. Yet that manic attention to petty detail is the very heart of the Islamists' program: it is only by getting all those details of beards and haircuts and veils right that Muslims will really be living as God has decreed, and only then will He help them to unite the whole Muslim world, defeat the West, and perhaps Islamize the planet. If Islamists gained power in an Arab country, they would be obliged by their beliefs to do the same. But Arabs are a good deal more sophisticated than Afghans, on average, and the idea of being subjected to the iron whim of Islamist fanatics did not appeal to most people at all. So although the Islamists' revolutionary adventure started with quite a bang, it quickly fizzled out.

In 1979, several hundred armed Islamists seized the Grand Mosque in Mecca and held it for two weeks before they were overwhelmed and killed. In 1981, Islamists assassinated President Anwar Sadat of Egypt. In 1982, the Muslim Brotherhood in Syria, a Sunni-based movement advocating a return to traditional Islamic principles, launched a full-scale uprising in Hama, and did not surrender until the city had been virtually levelled by the Syrian army. In each case, they expected their exemplary act of violence to trigger a nationwide uprising that would sweep the old regime away and bring them to power. In fact, in no case did the masses so much as stir. Support for the Islamist project was running at perhaps 5 per cent, at most 10 or 15 per cent, in the various Arab countries throughout the 1980s and 1990s, and if you cannot win mass support then you are never going to get to the end-game of the revolution.

Terrorism is fine for getting your name and your ideas out, since if you are blowing things up people will know who you are: the media, however closely controlled, *have* to talk about you, even if everything they say is lies. But the end-game of a revolutionary process usually requires huge mobs out in the streets defying death to bring the regime down and put you in power. (Another way to gain power is to have friends in the army willing to carry out a military coup for you, but that option was not available to the Islamists since Arab armies are generally quite careful about not letting Islamist officers rise to senior rank.)

Arabs are not fools, and most found it hard to believe that the solutions to all their problems were quite as simple as the Islamists contend. But if the Arab masses aren't willing to risk their lives to put the Islamist revolutionaries into power – if the mobs simply won't come out for them – then their revolutions never get off the ground. For the next twenty years the Islamist project was stalled: the Islamists occasionally killed some official or blew something up, but they were making no progress towards their first-stage goal of over-throwing Arab regimes. The later 1980s and the 1990s were a long and frustrating stalemate for the Islamists of the Arab world. The only place they even had a brief scent of success was in Algeria, where elections were cancelled in 1991 after main-stream Muslim "fundamentalist" parties looked like they were going to win. The Islamists quickly assumed the leadership of the rebels in the ensuing civil war, but the sheer barbarism of the Islamists' tactics and the extreme nature of their ideas eventually turned popular opinion against them, and after about 120,000 dead the war ended in an Islamist defeat. But there was one place where Arab Islamists really had made a difference: Afghanistan.

The Soviet Union had sent troops into Afghanistan in 1979 to defend a socialist military regime in Kabul from a U.S.-backed revolt by conservative hill tribesmen who hated the regime's modernizing measures: nobody was going to make *their* daughters go to school. But it was actually a trap: the United States had encouraged and armed the insurgents in the hope of luring the Russians into invading Afghanistan, the grave-yard of many previous invading armies. Once the Russians were in, the United States went all out to build up the resistance movement that quickly took shape: President Carter's national security adviser, Zbigniew Brzezinski, talked about creating "Russia's Vietnam." And part of building up the Afghan resist-ance was getting as many Arab Islamists as possible to go to Afghanistan and join the anti-Russian jihad. It got them out of the Arab countries, where they were a dangerous nuisance, and it gave the Afghan resistance some more sophisticated leader-ship, because Arab Islamists were mostly quite well-educated people and many had useful civilian skills like medical or engi-neering training.

Everybody knows about "blowback" now, but at the time there was quite a fashion among governments for using Islamists, who were seen as useful idiots. The Israeli govern-ment subsidized Hamas in the early days, thinking that it would be a handy counter-balance to the much more powerful secular wing of the Palestinian resistance movement, the Palestine Liberation Organization. Anwar Sadat was cultivat-ing Egyptian Islamists as a potential power base separate from the army until they killed him. And the United States had no compunction about supplying Arab Islamists in Afghanistan with weapons (Saudi Arabia paid most of their expenses) in the service of defeating the Russians. Which they and the Afghans duly did after ten years, but the "Arab Afghans" got something out of the deal, too. In fact, they got two things.

First, they got to know one another. Until all the young Arab Islamists went up to Afghanistan and spent years together fighting the Russians, they were stuck in their separate national compartments, knowing only the problems of being a revolutionary in Algeria or the iniquities of the regime in Syria. Just being all together, fighting in the same high cause of liberating Afghanistan from infidel occupation, gave them a broader perspective on the Arab world that they could never have learned from a whole lifetime spent dodging the Saudi or Moroccan police back home.

The other thing they acquired was a genuinely global perspective on how things worked. There they were, fighting the Russians, taking arms deliveries from the Americans, dealing on a regular basis with the Pakistani intelligence service, even talking to the Iranians from time to time: it was a crash course on how the game is played at the highest level, and they were good students. And then, after the Russians gave up and retreated from Afghanistan in 1989, leaving forty thousand dead, they had the time, sitting in their camps and in no hurry to go home to the Arab world (where many of them were wanted men), to consider how to put all this new knowledge to good use.

It was, by the accounts of those who were there, a time of intellectual ferment, with all sorts of strategies for breaking the deadlock that had paralyzed the Islamist cause in the Arab world being offered, considered, and dismissed. But the one that finally got traction and attracted the support of other respected leaders among the Arabs who had fought in Afghanistan was Osama bin Laden's proposal to create an organization that would concentrate exclusively on attacking the West (the United States, in fact) directly. Al-Qaeda was born from these debates, and from the start it was a very serious organization, dedicated to attacks that would seriously hurt the United States *in order to provoke American retaliation that would kill lots of innocent Muslims.* (The bit in italics, of course, was never discussed in public.)

A decade passed between the formation of al-Qaeda in Afghanistan and the attacks of September 2001. Bin Laden spent some time in Sudan, under a relatively friendly regime that was at least back in the Arab world, but after the Taliban won the civil war in 1996 he returned to Afghanistan and built his training camps there. The planning for the 9/11 operation began in late 1998, and bin Laden *must* have known that the United States would retaliate by invading Afghanistan. How could he not know that? But he was quite content that it should do so, because he expected that the Afghans would fight back in a long, brutal guerrilla war, as they had done when the Soviets invaded; and from that war would come a constant flow of images of innocent Afghan Muslims killed by American firepower that would decisively turn the Arab masses against their corrupt, oppressive, sold-out regimes and drive them into the arms of the revolutionaries. Critical mass would be achieved at last, the mobs would go down into the streets to overthrow the regimes, and our guys would finally get into power in major Arab countries.

That was his expectation, and the United States responded to the 9/11 attacks by invading Afghanistan. To that extent, his strategy succeeded. But the Bush administration did not do it in the good old-fashioned American military style, with several hundred thousand soldiers rolling into the country with immense firepower at their disposal and a better-safe-than-sorry attitude towards using it, while the air force blasted everything to ruins. Instead, it sent in only about five hundred special forces and CIA personnel, equipped with little more than large wads of cash, satellite phones, and laser-target designators. Their job was to buy up (or at least rent) the loyalty of the various ethnic militias belonging to the Northern Alliance, a loosely organized coalition of all the minority groups that were in rebellion against the Taliban government (which was drawn almost exclusively from the largest single ethnic group in Afghanistan, the Pashtuns).

No American army fought its way into Afghanistan. Most of America's major allies volunteered to send troops to help, and the entire operation was officially blessed post facto by the United Nations, but the actual fighting on the ground was done exclusively by the newly acquired local allies of the United States, while the U.S. Air Force helped them with precisely targeted bombing of Taliban positions (that was what the laser designators were for). At the point when Kabul, the capital, fell, in mid-November 2001, there were still probably fewer than a thousand Americans on the ground in the whole country. Total fatal casualties on all sides were probably under five thousand, which is a pretty small butcher's bill for taking down the government of a country of 25 million people. And as a result, there was no guerrilla war of resistance: the Taliban fled, bin Laden's camps were smashed and his fighters dispersed, and a modest army of occupation arrived to help restore stability and secure the process of installing a new, democratically elected government.

It had been, if one may use the word in such a context, an elegant operation, and as a result President Bush avoided the trap that bin Laden had laid for him. Most of the credit should probably go to the CIA and its director, George Tenet, who had this strategy up and running while the Pentagon was still fumbling with its plans, and the result was that by the end of 2001 Bush was in a position to go on television and tell the American public that the military phase of the "war on terror" was over. Police and intelligence operations to track down other al-Qaeda operatives would probably continue for years, but there were no more military targets: nowhere else did bin Laden's organization have government support and fixed bases.

He didn't say that. In January 2002, the month after the last resistance in Afghanistan had been quelled, Bush devoted his State of the Union speech to telling the American public about his discovery of the "axis of evil," and by the end of that speech it was quite clear that the United States was going to invade Iraq. Having cheated the Islamists of an easy success in Afghanistan, Bush then gave them a free kick, for the invasion of Iraq was everything that bin Laden had hoped the invasion of Afghanistan would be: 130,000 young U.S. soldiers fighting their way through a landscape filled with terrified civilians, calling on the enormous firepower available to them whenever there seemed to be a problem, and then a prolonged, in-your-face military occupation in which Americans with little knowledge of the country and none of the language ran everything – and ran it very badly. No wonder it blew up in their faces, and began producing a steady stream of images, from Abu Ghraib to Fallujah, that horrified Muslims everywhere. Bin Laden had no way of foreseeing the American invasion of Iraq, but it certainly has produced the radicalization of opinion in the Arab world that he had been hoping for.

"Iraq is now what Afghanistan was in the late-1970s and throughout the 80s into the 90s, and that's an insurgent magnet, if you will, a mujahedin magnet, only much, much worse."
　　　　　　　– Michael Scheuer, former head of the CIA's Bin Laden unit.
　　　　　　　　　　　　　　　　Quoted in *The Independent*, January 2005

All quite true, and yet, the revolutions in Arab countries that the Islamists have been striving for since the late 1970s have still not occurred. The United States has never been more disliked in the Arab world, and Arab regimes associated with it have a grave public relations problem at home, but there is no sign of a popular revolution brewing against even the most vulnerable regimes. That is not to say that they cannot happen, but we have had exactly the kind of situation that bin Laden had hoped to achieve for more than four years now, albeit in Iraq rather than Afghanistan, and the predicted results have not appeared. Perhaps his estimate of the volatility of Arab public opinion was over-optimistic.

Terrorist attacks in Western countries will doubtless continue in a minor key, probably carried out for the most part by young Muslims already living in those countries who have been radicalized by the invasion of Iraq, like the young British Muslims who carried out the July 2005 bombings on the London transport system. (The invasion of Afghanistan had less effect on Muslim opinion in Western countries, since there seemed some logical justification for it, whereas the lack of such a justification for invading Iraq left many in the Muslim diaspora convinced that there really was a concerted Western assault on Islam itself.)

"My Service needs to understand the motivations behind terrorism to succeed in countering it. . . . The video wills of British suicide bombers make it clear that they are motivated by perceived worldwide and long-standing injustices against Muslims . . . and their interpretation as anti-Muslim of U.K. foreign policy, in particular the U.K.'s involvement in Iraq and Afghanistan."

– Dame Eliza Manningham-Buller,
head of MI5 (British Intelligence), November 2006

The withdrawal of Western troops from both Iraq and Afghanistan would remove the main cause of this radicalization in Muslim communities in Western countries, however, and the likelihood of further attacks would then tend to diminish over time. As for genuinely international Islamist terrorism against Western countries that is planned and controlled from within the Muslim world, apart from 9/11 it has never been a significant phenomenon, and 9/11 increasingly looks like a one-off. Not only would it be much harder to carry out such an operation today in the face of much-improved security measures, but the strategic motive for doing so has dwindled drastically, since it would be very difficult to sucker the United States or other Western countries into invading Muslim countries again once the troops are out. If there should be another large attack, it is likelier to occur before the withdrawal, with a view to preventing it. An al-Qaeda video in late 2006 called President Bush a war criminal but pleaded with him not to withdraw American troops from the Middle East because "We haven't yet killed enough of them." A more honest commentary would have begged Bush not to withdraw the U.S. troops because they haven't yet killed enough Muslims to make the revolutions happen.

It remains to be seen, however, whether the new generation of Islamist jihadis created and hardened by the years of war in Iraq will actually succeed in overthrowing one or more Arab governments once the war ends and they turn their attention elsewhere. The goal of the movement from the start was to take power in Arab countries, and that has not changed.

CHAPTER VI

IRAN'S PUTATIVE BOMB

Tel Aviv, Jan. 3 – Iran is much closer to producing nuclear weapons than previously thought, and could be less than five years away from having an atomic bomb, several senior American and Israeli officials say.

"The date by which Iran will have nuclear weapons is no longer 10 years from now," a senior official said recently, referring to previous estimates. "If the Iranians maintain this intensive effort to get everything they need, they could have all their components in two years. Then it will be just a matter of technology and research. If Iran is not interrupted in this program by some foreign power, it will have the device in more or less five years."

The reassessment of Iran's nuclear potential is now described by Israeli officials as the most serious threat facing their country.

– The New York Times, January 5, 1995

I f this report had been correct, then Iran would have had
nuclear weapons in time for the millennium. If you go
back through the old newspaper archives, you can find a
similar report in practically any year of the past twenty.
Predicting that Iran is on the brink of getting nuclear weapons
is a well-established industry in Israel, and it has a fully owned
subsidiary in the United States. In 1992, for example, there was
a report by the Republican Research Committee of the U.S.
House of Representatives, obviously fed to them by Israel, that
there was a "98 per cent certainty" that Iran had bought at least
two Soviet-made nuclear warheads. Russia later said that the
warheads in question had been accounted for, but Israeli
officials refused to be reassured, suggesting that the warheads
might have gone to Iran, been disassembled and studied (a
process called "reverse engineering"), and then been returned
to Russia. If Iran had got nuclear weapons every time we
have been told it will have them within five years, it would have
hundreds of the things by now. But it doesn't. It has none. Only
Israel in the Middle East has hundreds of nuclear weapons, or
indeed any at all.

So why should we take the warnings about Iran any more
seriously this time? On January 18, 2007, Israeli historian Benny
Morris wrote in the *Jerusalem Post*, "One bright morning in five
or ten years, perhaps in a regional crisis, perhaps out of the blue,

a day or a year or five years after Iran's acquisition of the bomb, the mullahs in Qom will convene in secret session . . . and give President Mahmoud Ahmadinejad, by then in his second or third term, the go-ahead. The orders will go out and the Shihab III and IV missiles will take off for Tel Aviv, Beersheba, Haifa and Jerusalem. . . . Some of the Shihabs will be nuclear-tipped, perhaps even with multiple warheads. . . . With a country the size and shape of Israel (an elongated 20,000 square kilometers), probably four or five hits will suffice: No more Israel. A million or more Israelis in the greater Tel Aviv, Haifa and Jerusalem areas will die immediately. Millions will be seriously irradiated. Israel has about seven million inhabitants. No Iranian will see or touch an Israeli. It will be quite impersonal."

It was a deliberately blood-curdling vision – Morris called his piece "This Holocaust will be different" – but one wonders why the Iranians would do as he suggests, knowing that their own people would immediately suffer the identical fate under a rain of several hundred Israeli nuclear weapons. Who truly believes that Mahmoud Ahmadinejad will even be president of Iran in five or ten years' time?

Morris's device for making his scenario seem credible is simply to insist that Iranians, being devout Muslims, are beyond the reach of reason (he uses the phrase "mad mullahs" several times). This kind of apocalyptic panic-mongering is a recurrent strand in Israeli political discourse, but it's hard for most other people to take it seriously: it's Israel that has the nuclear weapons. True, the United Nations has now been persuaded to impose sanctions on Iran (although quite mild ones), on suspicion that it is trying to develop its own nukes, and the United States declares that "all options are on the table" and moves its forces around in a menacing manner. But there are no Iranian nuclear weapons now, nor is it certain that there ever will be.

The origin of the current crisis over an alleged Iranian nuclear weapons program was intelligence received in 2002 from an Iranian opposition group, the National Council of Resistance of Iran (NCRI), that the country was building a secret uranium-enrichment facility at Natanz and a heavy-water plant at Arak, both a few hours' drive south of Tehran. The NCRI is a political front for the outlawed Mujahideen-e-Khalq (MEK), a Marxist revolutionary organization that has spent two decades fighting the Shah in Iran and another quarter-century fighting the ayatollahs. MEK is classified by both the United States and the European Union as a terrorist organization, and it regularly seeks to discredit the Iranian government, but this time the report was largely correct. There was a heavy-water plant being built at Arak, to supply a forty MW heavy-water reactor that is to be built there by 2014. More ominously, there was indeed a large facility at Natanz designed to house the high-speed centrifuges that are used to enrich uranium, whether for use in nuclear power reactors or in nuclear weapons, and it had been under construction for eighteen years.

That's the first signal that there may be less going on here than meets the eye. They've been working on Natanz for eighteen years and they still don't have the first centrifuges running? Can Iranian workmen be that slow? And what was going on back in 1984, when they allegedly started work? Oh, yes, the Iran–Iraq war.

A little background. The Shah of Iran, whom the United States and Britain boosted into absolute power in a 1953 coup that removed a democratically elected government, began building nuclear power stations in the 1970s with the open blessing of Washington. He also had its tacit assent to an

Iranian nuclear weapons program, because Iran was being groomed as the new pro-Western great power that would be America's policeman in the Middle East. But it was not to be.

When the Iranian revolution of 1979 overthrew the Shah, the leader of the new Islamic Republic of Iran, Ayatollah Ruhollah Khomeini, cancelled the nuclear weapons program on the grounds that "weapons of mass destruction" are un-Islamic. He retained the nuclear power program, but that also ground to a halt when Saddam Hussein's Iraq invaded Iran (with U.S. encouragement) in 1980. Hundreds of thousands of Iranian casualties later, in 1984, with clear evidence that Saddam was working on nuclear weapons, Iran apparently decided it had better get them too, un-Islamic or not, for that was when construction began on the Natanz facility.

The war ended four years later, however, and the urgency went out of the program. Two years after that, in 1990, Saddam Hussein invaded Kuwait (possibly under the misapprehension that he had the permission of the United States), and was soundly defeated in the Gulf War. After the war, UN arms inspectors combed Iraq for forbidden weapons and comprehensively dismantled Saddam's nuclear weapons program – whereupon Iran appears to have stopped work on the Natanz facility entirely. It would still be useful for enriching uranium to the much lower level required for nuclear power reactors, but there was certainly no hurry about that, as the only two large reactors under construction in the country, light-water German-designed models at Bushehr, had been badly damaged by Iraqi air raids during the war. During the middle and late 1990s, there appears to have been no work whatever done on uranium enrichment in Iran.

At no point did Iran report the Natanz site to the International Atomic Energy Agency (IAEA), which inspects the nuclear facilities of countries that have signed the Nuclear Non-Proliferation Treaty (NPT). However, it was under no legal obligation to do so, as its agreement with the IAEA specified that new facilities must be reported six months before actual nuclear material is introduced into them, and neither Natanz (nor the later facility at Arak) had reached that stage when the Mujahideen-e-Khalq spilled the beans in 2002. Why did it not declare the existence of Natanz long ago anyway? Perhaps because of security considerations: it began the work when Iraqi air raids were a daily event, and subsequently had to work around a U.S. trade embargo that included severe American pressure on other potential suppliers of sensitive technologies to Iran. Why ask for trouble before you have to?

It is not clear when exactly work resumed at Natanz, but it was almost certainly in 1999 or 2000. The official Iranian explanation is that they have decided on an enormous expansion of nuclear power generation, and want to control every part of the process from uranium mine to reactor so as not to be vulnerable to embargoes and similar external problems. It is not inherently unbelievable that a country with as much oil as Iran would want nuclear reactors too: both Russia and Canada have invested heavily in nuclear power although they are major oil exporters. Even Iran's desire to have the complete nuclear fuel cycle under its own control is not unreasonable, as many other signatories of the NPT do the same. But the decision does raise some questions, particularly given the timing.

The Israelis, as always, think it is about them, and the United States, as usual, shares their view, but there is good reason to suspect that it was really Pakistan's nuclear tests in 1998 that got the Iranian nuclear program moving again. Pakistan, a country with twice Iran's population and its neighbour to the east, was politically a reasonably predictable quantity at that time, and its nuclear weapons were clearly aimed at India, not Iran. However, Pakistan's population is almost 80 per cent Sunni Muslim, and it is home to more radical Islamists than any other non-Arab country. There are even some Islamic extremists who have been promoted to senior ranks in the armed forces, so there was already room for concern in Iranians' minds.

In the following year, 1999, the democratically elected government of Pakistan was overthrown by the military under the leadership of General Pervez Musharraf, who has remained in power ever since. He, too, is a predictable quantity and no extremist, but Pakistan now has a one-bullet regime – and twice already Musharraf has only narrowly escaped assassination. So any morning Shia Iran could wake up to find that its next-door neighbour has fallen under the control of Sunni fanatics with nuclear weapons. In that situation, any prudent person might start thinking about appropriate precautions.

Iran's president in 1999 was Mohammad Khatami, universally regarded as a moderate and a reformer, and the whole political trend in the country was towards liberalization at home and reconciliation abroad. There were even political feelers extended towards the United States, and in 2001 Iran co-operated unreservedly with the U.S. invasion of Afghanistan after the atrocity of 9/11. It was not a time when Iran was looking for a fight with either the West or even Israel (where the "peace process" with the Palestinians had not yet broken down). The final decision on whether or not to adopt a course that might ultimately lead to Iranian nuclear weapons would have belonged to the unelected religious authorities – the Supreme Leader, Ayatollah Ali Khamenei, and the twelve-man Council of Guardians – and not to the elected president, but Ayatollah Khamenei has publicly repeated the late Ayatollah Khomeini's condemnation of weapons of mass destruction as un-Islamic, and we may assume that he takes his own religious decrees seriously. So the decision that was taken in 1999 was probably quite modest and rational.

Iran did not need nuclear weapons in 1999. The only two countries it might want to deter from a nuclear attack were Israel and the United States, and neither seemed remotely likely to launch such an attack. Israel had probably had nuclear weapons targeted on Iran for thirty years already, and by the 1990s it undoubtedly had the capacity to destroy all of Iran's cities and kill half the population in a single day, but that was a familiar danger and the Israelis weren't crazy. The same went for the United States: nobody ever decided to get nuclear weapons out of fear of Bill Clinton. On the other hand, Pakistan, while it was not a threat at the moment, could suddenly turn very scary indeed – so what Iran needed was not nuclear weapons now, but the ability to build them in a hurry if the situation changed.

It's called a "threshold" nuclear weapons capability in the trade, and it's much more widespread than you might think. All you need is the ability to enrich uranium in industrial quantities, which is quite legal under the Nuclear Non-Proliferation Treaty and perfectly justifiable if you want an independent source of fuel for your nuclear reactors. The IAEA will send inspectors around from time to time to ensure that you aren't enriching uranium up to weapons grade (about 90 per cent pure) instead of industrial grade (20 per cent or less), but if you ever change your mind and decide that you need nuclear weapons fast, you just quit the NPT and run the uranium through the same centrifuges more times. Once you have enough weapons-grade uranium, it should take no more than six months to a year to build functioning nuclear weapons from the word *go* (provided you have done your scientific homework in advance). It's a two-way bet that you cannot lose.

That is probably the decision that Iran really made in 1999: to build the enrichment facility now, but to go for nuclear weapons only when there was a real panic about Pakistan (or somewhere else) in the future. Many other countries (for example, Brazil, Germany, and Australia) have made the same decision, built the full nuclear fuel cycle that gives them "threshold" status, and never taken the final step. Iran has broken no rules, and none stand in the way of its completing the work at Natanz and accomplishing its short-term goal. That will automatically give it the ability to build nuclear weapons if it chooses to abandon the NPT at some later date, but this is a flaw inherent in the NPT's original design.

It is easy to be cynical about the NPT, one of the most curious treaties ever signed. In order to prevent the proliferation of nuclear weapons beyond the five countries that already had them in 1968, those five – the United States, the Soviet Union (Russia), the United Kingdom, France, and China – agreed to "pursue plans to reduce and liquidate their stockpiles," and eventually to conclude "a Treaty on general and complete disarmament under strict and effective international control." None of them had the slightest intention of doing such a thing, of course, and forty years later most of them are happily working away on their next generation of nuclear weapons. So how did they get almost all the other countries in the world to sign the NPT? By extending the carrot of international assistance for all members that want to develop civilian nuclear power generation – *including uranium enrichment and fuel reprocessing capabilities, which automatically confer the ability to develop nuclear weapons.* Promise not to build the bombs, and we'll promise to give you the means.

So signatories of the NPT can all build fuel-enrichment facilities, ostensibly to provide fuel for their power-generating reactors, and the IAEA will conclude an agreement with each one that includes periodic inspections to ensure that no fuel is being enriched beyond the appropriate level or diverted to non-civilian uses. The IAEA will even provide technical assistance for countries that are having trouble solving some of the more demanding technical problems involved in the process. And if any of those countries should subsequently change its mind and decide that it must have nuclear weapons, it can withdraw from the NPT after giving three months' notice. Any country that is prepared to lie its head off about its ultimate intentions can therefore use the NPT's provisions as cover and justification for its nuclear weapons program until the last few months, then "break out" of the treaty and go public with the bomb.

Given this gigantic loophole in the treaty, it is remarkable that only one country has availed itself of it. Four of the five countries that have acquired nuclear weapons since 1968 were honest enough never to sign the NPT at all: Israel, India, Pakistan, and South Africa (which built six nuclear weapons in the 1980s but subsequently dismantled them all and signed the

NPT in 1991). Only one country, North Korea, signed the NPT but subsequently withdrew (2003) and tested a nuclear weapon (October 2006). According to the head of the IAEA, Mohamed ElBaradei, forty other countries that have signed the NPT are capable of making the material needed for a nuclear bomb, including Australia, Canada, and all the larger Latin American countries, sixteen European countries, Algeria and Egypt among the Arab countries, and Bangladesh, Indonesia, Japan, South Korea, and Vietnam in Asia. Iran just wants to be the forty-first.

"There are many reasons why Iran is seeking nuclear power. The history of our nuclear activity dates back 45 years to the time of the ex-shah's regime. But after the Islamic revolution, some western countries condemned Iran and cancelled their nuclear agreements with us. For example, the Americans had concluded an agreement for a research reactor in Tehran and also to provide the fuel. But they cancelled the agreement and did not give back the money. The Germans did the same. So the lesson was: we have to be self-sufficient, to provide fuel for ourselves.

"We don't see why we should stop the scientific research of our country. We understand why this is very sensitive, but they [the West] are categorising countries. Some countries can have access to high nuclear technology. The others are told they can produce fruit juice and pears! They say: 'Don't seek a nuclear bomb.' We don't have any objection to that. But unfortunately officials of some countries . . . say, 'We don't want you to have the knowledge for nuclear technology.' This is not logical. And we don't pay attention to this."

– Ali Larijani, secretary of the Supreme National Security Council and chief Iranian negotiator on nuclear issues, interview in *The Guardian*, August 21, 2006

It really is a question of trust, in the end. What Iran was doing in 2002 was not illegal, and it promptly suspended work at Natanz and other sites that had raised suspicion that it was breaking the rules – a voluntary suspension that ultimately lasted for three years. But both Israel and the United States were profoundly suspicious of Iran's intentions, and pressed the IAEA to investigate the matter very aggressively.

Israel's concern was that nuclear weapons in any Muslim country in the region would break the monopoly that allows Israel to make implicit threats of using them against neighbouring countries without fear of retaliation, and could even endanger Israel itself if the Muslim country in question were controlled by suicidal maniacs. (So it is Israeli policy always to portray any country in the region with nuclear aspirations as being under the control of suicidal maniacs.) Deterrence has worked in only one direction in the Middle East for the past forty years, and that is an advantage that Israel does not want to lose. As Moshe Sneh, a leading Israeli strategist, put it, "I don't want the Israeli-Palestinian negotiations to be held under the shadow of an Iranian nuclear bomb." (The fact that they are always held under the shadow of hundreds of Israeli bombs does not cause him equal concern.)

The U.S. concern is partly on Israel's behalf, but also partly on behalf of its Arab allies in the Gulf and beyond, all of whom would be very unhappy about the existence of an Iranian bomb when there is no Arab bomb. The Arab–Iranian split is many centuries old and the mutual suspicion is deeply ingrained. But that does not begin to compare with the poisonous cloud of mistrust that has hung over the U.S.–Iranian relationship for the past fifty years.

The Iranians have neither forgotten nor forgiven the American-backed 1953 coup that launched the quarter-century tyranny of the Shah, nor U.S. encouragement of Saddam Hussein's invasion of Iran in 1980 and the help that Washington gave to Iraq during the war, nor President Bush's inclusion of Iran in his "axis of evil" speech in 2002. The U.S. government cannot forgive Iranians for overthrowing the Shah, its closest ally in the Middle East, nor for the hostage-taking at the U.S. embassy in Tehran just after the revolution that kept fifty-two American diplomats and others imprisoned for fifteen months, nor the way U.S. forces were driven out of Lebanon in 1983 by Iranian-backed truck bombers, nor for backing Hezbollah in Lebanon to this day. Washington eventually accepted Muammar Gaddafi's apology for carrying out terrorist attacks and trying to get nuclear weapons without seeking to remove the Libyan dictator, and it even sat down at the same table with the North Koreans after they had actually tested a nuclear bomb, but it finds it very hard to do the same with Iran. Only with Cuba does the United States have such a pathological relationship (including an American embargo), perhaps in both cases because the other government has *successfully* defied Washington.

In May 2003, the Iranian government, shocked by the easy U.S. conquest of Iraq and the sudden arrival of American armed forces on its western border (they were already on its eastern border with Afghanistan), sent a message to the U.S. State Department proposing a global settlement of all the disputes between the two countries. It arrived in Washington on May 2, 2003, just before a meeting in Geneva between Iran's UN ambassador, Javad Zarif, and neo-conservative star Zalmay Khalilzad, then a senior director at the National Security Council and now

U.S. ambassador to the UN. According to the account of Trita Parsi of the Carnegie Endowment for International Peace (supplemented by a report by Gareth Porter in the *American Prospect* and confirmed by Iranian and former U.S. officials), Iran offered to take "decisive action against any terrorists (above all, al-Qaeda) in Iranian territory," in exchange for U.S. cooperation in pursuing "anti-Iranian terrorists" – i.e., the Mujahideen-e-Khalq. Iran insisted on its right to "full access to peaceful nuclear technology," but would submit to much stricter inspections by adopting "all relevant instruments (. . . and all further IAEA protocols)," thus giving IAEA monitors no-notice access to any Iranian facility they wanted to inspect, including ones that had not been declared by Iran.

Most importantly, Tehran offered to join with moderate Arab regimes such as Egypt and Jordan in accepting the 2002 Arab League Beirut declaration that called for peace with Israel in return for Israel's withdrawal to its pre-1967 borders. It would work to change the Hezbollah guerrilla organization into a mere "political organization within Lebanon," and it would end "any material support to Palestinian opposition groups (Hamas, Islamic Jihad, etc.) from Iranian territory." It would even bring pressure to bear on these organizations "to stop violent actions against civilians within Israel's 1967 borders." All the United States had to do in return was renew diplomatic ties with Iran, end sanctions, and "recognise Iran's legitimate security interests in the region with according defense capacity." The offer had the support of both Supreme Leader Ali Khamenei and then-president Mohammad Khatami, respectively the heads of Iran's clerical and secular governments. But the Bush administration rejected the Iranian approach as casually as it had ignored Saddam Hussein's desperate last-minute offer to admit American troops to Iraq, with unlimited access to suspected WMD sites, only a few months before. "We're not interested in any grand bargain," said John Bolton, then undersecretary of state for arms control and international security.

This was during the time when the neo-conservatives and nationalists around Bush felt utterly omnipotent, and Iran (and Syria) were next on the hit list. They were convinced that the Iranian regime was on its last legs and would fall at the first strong push. So the United States pressured the IAEA to find evidence of work on illegal weapons in Iran, and the IAEA duly followed up all the various leads about secret nuclear weapons sites provided by the U.S. intelligence services, but all the tips led to dead ends: "They gave us a paper with a list of sites ... but there was no sign of [banned nuclear] activities," said a diplomat at IAEA headquarters in Vienna, reported in the *Guardian* on February 23, 2007. "Now [the inspectors] don't go in blindly. Only if it passes a credibility test." And meanwhile, Iran's right to develop the full nuclear fuel cycle became a *cause célèbre* and nationalist rallying point in Iranian domestic politics.

By August 2005, the IAEA still hadn't found anything, and in Tehran the fear of American power had turned into a realization that U.S. troops were in deep trouble in Iraq. So Iran called in the IAEA observers and removed the seals that it had placed on its own enrichment facilities three years before, implicitly defying the United States to do anything about it. There was no chance of getting further action out of the IAEA against Iran, as many other NPT signatories that were also enriching fuel, including powerful states like Brazil, South Korea, and Japan, were concerned that imposing sanctions merely on the suspicion that a member wanted to develop nuclear weapons would have a legal impact on their own rapidly growing civil nuclear power programs. Instead, at the initiative of the United States, the issue was transferred to the UN Security Council, where the great powers have more clout. And just at this point, the Iranians made the serious mistake of electing Mahmoud Ahmadinejad to the presidency.

It was almost an accident. Ahmadinejad was the darkest of dark horses among the eleven presidential candidates, having never held any office higher than mayor of Tehran. But his rivals were so unappetizing – several more attractive candidates having been purged from the list by the Guardian Council of ayatollahs as insufficiently Islamic – that he ended up in the run-off between the two leading candidates, and then his populist approach and man-of-the-people demeanour carried him on to victory. The vote was really a protest by rural people and the pious poor against the corruption of the religious and political elite who dominate the Islamic Republic and the perceived retreat from "Islamic values" under the outgoing president. What the voters got, however, was an arch-conservative and religious fanatic – he firmly believes in the imminent return of the "Hidden Imam," the Shia equivalent of Christians who await the Rapture any day now – who has repeatedly embarrassed the Iranian regime with his ever-open mouth. For an educated man, Ahmadinejad is remarkably ignorant, and he completely lacks the self-discipline that senior officers of the state must exercise in their public statements.

Ahmadinejad's greatest blunder came early in his presidency, in a speech to a students' conference entitled "World Without Zionism" in October 2005, when he quoted the founder of the Islamic Republic as follows (according to the translation published in the *New York Times*): "Our dear imam [referring to Ayatollah Khomeini] said that the occupying regime [Israel] must be wiped off the map and this was a very wise statement." This was instantly seized upon by Israel and others as an incitement to genocide, and has been used ever since as evidence that Iran is a clone of Hitler's Germany, developing nuclear weapons solely so that it can exterminate the Jewish people. At the 2006 conference of the American Israel Public Affairs Committee, probably the most powerful single-issue political lobby in the United States, huge screens cut back and forth between Ahmadinejad making the alleged "wiped off the map" remark and a clip of a ranting Adolf Hitler. The campaign has been so effective that more than half the references to Ahmadinejad that I have seen in the international press during my research, and an even larger proportion of those that refer directly to Iran's alleged nuclear weapons program, directly quote him as calling for Israel to be wiped from the map.

The truth is somewhat different. Ahmadinejad's speech was recorded, and a subsequent translation by Dr. Juan Cole, professor of Middle Eastern and South Asian history at the University of Michigan, offers this version of the offending statement: "The imam said that this regime occupying Jerusalem must [vanish from] the pages of time." It was quite clear from the context of the speech that Ahmadinejad was actually calling for an end to the "Zionist regime" in Israel, not for the extermination of the Jewish people: other examples he gave of apparently invincible regimes that have vanished from the pages of time included the Soviet Union, Saddam Hussein's regime in Iraq, and the Shah's regime in Iran itself. In every case, it was the regime that disappeared, not the people it ruled, and two of those three transitions did not involve military action.

Neither Ahmadinejad, nor the long-dead Ayatollah Khomeini whom he was quoting, has ever called for the extermination of Israel's Jews, nor indeed has either of them ever said that the passing of the Zionist regime in Israel was imminent, or that Iran would be directly involved in it – and in a damage-limitation exercise the following month, Iran's Supreme Leader, Ayatollah Khamenei, stressed that Iran's objection was to an exclusive state for the Jews in part of Palestine, not to the presence of Jews in the region:

"Several decades ago, Egyptian statesman Gamal Abdel Nasser, who was the most popular Arab personality, stated in his slogans that the Egyptians would throw the Jewish usurpers of Palestine into the sea. Some years later, Saddam Hussein, the most hated Arab figure, said that he would put half of the Palestinian land [i.e., Israel] on fire. But we would not approve of either of these two remarks.

"We believe, according to our Islamic principles, that neither throwing the Jews into the sea nor putting the Palestinian land on fire is logical and reasonable. . . . We have suggested that all native Palestinians, whether they are Muslims, Christians or Jews, should be allowed to take part in a general referendum before the eyes of the world and decide on a Palestinian government. Any government that is the result of this referendum will be a legitimate government."

– Ayatollah Khamenei's speech to government officials,
November 4, 2005

It was the familiar "one-state" solution, in which everybody who lives within the boundaries of the former British mandate of Palestine, plus refugees and the descendants of refugees from there, would have the right to vote on the future of a single state in that space (and the Arab Palestinians, including all the refugees, would outnumber the Jews and decide its future). After the grown-ups jerked Ahmadinejad's choke-chain, he, too, explicitly espoused this formula, telling *Time* magazine: "Our suggestion is that the five million Palestinian refugees come back to their homes, and then the entire people on those lands hold a referendum and choose their own system of government. This is a democratic and popular way."

It was all far too late. Just as Soviet premier Nikita Khrushchev's famous remark of 1956, "We will bury you," was deliberately misused for decades afterwards by Western hawks to prove the aggressive intentions of the Soviet Union (what Khrushchev actually said was: "Whether you like it or not, history is on our side. We will bury you"), so Ahmadinejad's remark will be used for many years as evidence that Iran wants nuclear weapons so that it can commit genocide against Israel. And Ahmadinejad is still the loosest of cannons: his own website translates his notorious remarks into English as a call to "wipe [Israel] from the map," and he promotes Holocaust denial as well. In a sense it doesn't really matter much what he thinks, since the elected president of Iran has no power over nuclear policy or foreign policy – under Iran's bizarre dual system of power, both those areas are the exclusive province of the unelected, religious Supreme Leader – but he is Israel's best weapon in the propaganda battle for world public opinion, and Iran's enemies use the weapon almost daily.

"The Iranian president has stated his desire to destroy our ally, Israel. So when you start listening to what he has said, to their desire to develop a nuclear weapon, then you begin to see an issue of grave national security concern."

– President George W. Bush, March 10, 2006

"Iran openly, explicitly and publicly threatens to wipe Israel off the map. Can you say that this is the same level – when they are aspiring to have nuclear weapons – as America, France, Israel, Russia?"
　　　　　– Israeli prime minister Ehud Olmert, December 11, 2006

Ehud Olmert was heavily criticized in Israel for this statement, contrasting responsible nuclear weapons powers like America, France, Israel, and Russia with irresponsible Iran, as Israeli leaders are never supposed to stray from the formula of "strategic ambiguity" in which they neither confirm nor deny the existence of Israel's nuclear weapons. (Another recent blunder of the same sort was Vice-Premier Shimon Peres's remark in May 2006: "The president of Iran should remember that Iran can also be wiped off the map.") But there is no question that Iran has lost the public relations battle, thanks largely to Ahmadinejad, and that it will end up in a political confrontation with the "international community" – i.e., the developed countries of the West – and perhaps in a military confrontation with Israel and/or the United States, if it continues to pursue the capability to enrich uranium. You cannot prove a negative, and Tehran will never now persuade most outsiders that its quest for a full nuclear fuel cycle under Iranian control is not really just a cover for a nuclear weapons program. And perhaps the outsiders are right, though it is probably just seeking a "threshold" capability for the time being. So where do we go from here?

"[The buildup to an attack on Iran] is absolutely parallel [to Iraq]. They're using the same dance steps – demonize the bad guys, the

pretext of diplomacy, keep out of negotiations, use proxies. It is Iraq redux."

– Philip Giraldi, former CIA counterterrorism expert.
Quoted by Craig Unger, *Vanity Fair*, March 2007

The principal strategic effect of the U.S. invasion of Iraq has been to make Iran the new regional great power, which is quite the opposite of what Washington and its Israeli allies intended. "The U.S., with coalition help, has eliminated two of Iran's regional rival governments – the Taliban in Afghanistan and Saddam Hussein's regime in Iraq – but has failed to replace either with coherent and stable political structures," concluded the Royal Institute of International Affairs (Chatham House) in a study in August 2006, adding that Iranian influence in Iraq is now greater than that of the United States, and that Iran is also a "prominent presence" in Afghanistan. The only conceivable way for Washington to reverse this unsought outcome in the short run is to inflict a severe military defeat on Iran. If the United States does attack Iran, reducing Iran's newly acquired power in the region will be its primary motive.

On December 23, 2006, the UN Security Council imposed modest sanctions on Iran for disobeying a previous Security Council order to stop enrichment operations – a ban on the supply of specified materials and technology that could contribute to Iran's missile and nuclear programs, and an asset freeze on certain companies and individuals involved in those programs – but Russian and Chinese support for this resolution did not come from a genuine fear of Iranian nuclear weapons. Like the planners in Washington, those in Moscow and Beijing know that there is no imminent threat from Iranian nuclear weapons. IAEA director general Mohamed

ElBaradei told the *Financial Times* on February 19, 2007, that "the intelligence, the British intelligence, the American intelligence, is that Iran is still years, five to ten years, away from developing a weapon."

What the Russians, the Chinese, and others on the Security Council were really trying to do was placate the United States and stave off a military confrontation in the Gulf, but it may not work. Many informed sources insist that the United States may attack Iran anyway, and some fear that it might even include attacks with tactical nuclear weapons against the deeply buried and hardened sites of the Iranian enrichment program. When former British foreign secretary Jack Straw exclaimed in April 2006 that such an attack would be "completely nuts" – and lost his job the following month, perhaps for *lèse-amérique* – it was widely assumed in Britain that he had just heard that the nuclear attacks were actually going to happen.

The U.S. defence budget is more than a hundred times bigger than Iran's, but a lower-cost economy means that Iran can afford lots of soldiers (475,000 regular troops and Revolutionary Guards), so a land invasion on a major scale is not an option for the United States. On the other hand, most Iranian air defences are not capable of coping with modern U.S. electronics, so the United States can bomb when and where and how much it wishes. Just 120 B52, B1, and B2 bombers are able to hit five thousand targets on a single mission, and Iran's political, military, and economic infrastructure (except oil) would probably be targeted in addition to nuclear-related targets, so one day's bombing could do more damage than Iran could repair in a year. Despite its heavy troop commitments in Iraq, the United States does still have enough special forces and other ground troops available to be able to seize coastal oil fields and conduct other raids into Iran, and there are persistent reports that American agents have been seeking allies among the large Azerbaijani, Kurdish, Arab, Turkoman and Baluchi minorities who live in Iran's border areas.

However, there is no obvious way in which the United States could bring the war to a victorious conclusion unless (as some in Washington fondly hope) American attacks unleash a revolt against the current regime in Iran and not a surge of patriotic fervour. The use of tactical nuclear weapons on hardened targets would not force Iranians to surrender (although it would have grave long-term implications for the safety of the world). Indeed, Richard Clarke, who served as a counter-terrorism adviser in the White House under three administrations, recalled in the *New York Times* of April 16, 2006, that in the 1990s the Clinton administration considered a bombing campaign against Iran, but that "after a long debate, the highest levels of the military could not forecast a way in which things would end favourably for the United States." Things have not changed, and there are no good military options for the United States.

In particular, the U.S. Navy could lose significant numbers of ships in the shallow, relatively narrow waters of the Persian Gulf if it tried to hold it open for tanker shipping, because one military area in which Iranian technology (or rather, Russian technology bought by Iran) is just as good as American technology is long-range sea-skimming missiles. (A similar missile, probably supplied to Hezbollah by Iran, gave the Israeli navy a nasty surprise during the recent war in Lebanon.) U.S. troops in both Iraq and Afghanistan could expect many problems as Iran helped the local anti-occupation forces, and American troops in central and northern Iraq could simply be cut off if

Shia militias in the south closed the few highways along which the Americans' supplies arrive from supply bases in Kuwait.

But let us leave this foolishness and consider what the consequences would be if neither the United States nor Israel attacks the Islamic Republic of Iran. Will Iran overrun the Gulf? Will it unleash subversion against the governments of the Arab states to the south? Will it simply absorb Iraq, or at least most of it? Will it attack Israel?

A physical advance by a large Iranian force even into Iraq, let alone farther afield, is extremely unlikely. The Iranians, having watched the Americans' difficulties in occupying Iraq, would not wish to repeat them, and in any case the Iranian armed forces lack the logistical ability to support a large force at any distance from the country's borders. This is not a cutting-edge, twenty-first-century force, although it would probably do quite well in defensive operations.

Subversion and destabilization, mainly via the disadvantaged Shia minorities who live in most of the Arab states along the southern and western shores of the Gulf, is certainly a tool available to the Iranian government, and in some cases it could be an effective one – but this tool has always been available, and Iran has used it sparingly, if at all, in the past. The question, then as now, is: Why would Iran want to destabilize its own neighbourhood? It is never going to absorb those Sunni-majority, Arabic-speaking countries, so there is no profit in it. It does not want Sunni Islamists to come to power there, for they are the Shias' worst enemies. Its best bet would be to stick with the existing regimes but to urge them warmly to get rid of the American military presence on their soil. (There is currently at least some U.S. military presence in almost every Gulf sheikhdom and kingdom between Kuwait and Oman.) If the

United States actually launches a war against Iran, most of these countries would desperately try to stay out of it, which would probably involve asking the Americans to leave. If it doesn't, they may still decide that that's a good idea.

Iran is never going to absorb Iraq: it has quite enough restive Arabic-speakers in Khuzestan province already. Nor would even Shia Iraqis welcome such a proposal, if it were to be made. The only Arab borders that are at risk of changing are on Iraq's western and southern frontiers, not its eastern one.

And will Iran attack Israel? Certainly not before it gets nuclear weapons, which could be in five years' time, or ten years, or never, for there is no common border on which it could fight a land war with Israel. Even with nuclear weapons of its own, any Iranian government that was not entirely mad would still be deterred from attacking by Israel's far larger number of nuclear weapons, and despite what its enemies would have us believe Iran has never had such a government. The main negative effect of Iranian nuclear weapons would be the pressure they created for the larger Arab states to get them too – and even smaller ones: in December 2006, the six members of the Gulf Cooperation Council – Bahrain, Kuwait, Oman, Qatar, Saudi Arabia, and the United Arab Emirates – announced a joint nuclear energy development project. If they really are concerned about energy, then it makes Iran's argument for nuclear energy even more convincing, for these are the countries with the highest ratio of oil production to population in the world. And if they are also taking out some insurance against possible Iranian nuclear weapons, in the familiar cascade model of proliferation – Pakistan got nuclear weapons because of India's, Iran seeks them out of fear of Pakistan's, the Gulf states get them out of fear of Iran's – then at the end of the road they face an existential crisis, because the country that will panic if they go nuclear is not Iran but Israel.

Despite its revolutionary rhetoric, Iran is essentially a status quo power, especially in its foreign policy, and whatever vestiges of revolutionary enthusiasm Mahmoud Ahmadinejad brings to the scene are likely to depart with him. That may not be too long in the future, although his current term runs until 2009, for even his allies in the Majlis (parliament) are talking of impeaching him, and the Supreme Leader can dismiss him at any time. He has been as irresponsible in domestic affairs as in his remarks about international issues, and the Iranian economy is failing despite the surge in oil revenues driven by higher prices.

Iran today is a very different country than it was at the time of the revolution in 1979. Then, more than half the population was illiterate and almost two-thirds were rural. Now Iran has twice as many people, 75 million, but most are city-dwellers and literacy is 80 per cent. Iranians in their twenties and thirties are less politically active than their parents' generation, but they expect a much higher standard of living, and they get grumpy if the government fails to deliver it. Ahmadinejad's commitment to "put the oil wealth on the tables of the poor" through direct government subsidies – everything from aid to poor areas to housing loans for newlyweds – raised government spending by 21 per cent in 2006 and triggered a sharp burst of inflation that has actually cut everybody's living standards: food prices soared in Iran in 2006, and house prices and rents in Tehran rose 50 per cent in only the last six months of the year. At the same time, his loose talk about Israel made it easier for the United States to obtain UN sanctions against Iran, and to persuade Iran's European and Japanese trading partners (there is almost no direct U.S.–Iran trade) to restrict their dealings with the Tehran regime. Foreign credits are drying up, foreign trade is dropping, and unemployment, officially 12 per cent when Ahmadinejad took office but in reality much higher, has not improved. His presidency is in deep trouble, and one of the few things that might save him is a U.S. attack.

The larger economic picture in Iran is also grim. In 1974, Iran produced 6.1 million barrels of oil a day; now, thanks to decades of gross under-investment, it produces only 3.9 million b/d. In September 2006, Oil Minister Kazem Vaziri-Hamaneh estimated that without new investment, oil production would fall by about 13 per cent a year, but little of that investment will come from outside in current circumstances. Eighty per cent of the economy is state-owned or controlled, and there is chronic looting by the arch-conservative clerical elite who have manoeuvred themselves into positions of power in those institutions. Although the Supreme Leader is not thought to be personally involved in this corruption, his disrespectful popular nickname, "Ali Shah," is a measure of popular disillusionment with the current regime. Most people will close ranks around the regime if Iran is attacked, for Iranians are nothing if not patriotic, but left to their own devices they may in time find ways of forcing it to change.

And there is probably plenty of time, because Iran's technological resources are pretty marginal for the task of creating a full nuclear cycle, let alone actual nuclear weapons, without substancial foreign assistance. It will doubtless solve all the technical problems in the end, but this is enrichment on a shoestring, and there will be no early breakthroughs.

Roger Stern of Johns Hopkins University in Baltimore put it

best: "The mullahs are doing a good job of destroying Iran's economy. They should be left alone to complete their work. Attacking Iran would allow the regime to escape responsibility for the economic disaster it created. . . . For these reasons, the best policy towards Iran may be to do nothing at all." (*International Herald Tribune*, January 8, 2007)

It would have been good advice for Iraq, too.

CHAPTER VII

NOT THE SHIA CRESCENT,
THE ISLAMIST REVOLUTIONARIES

"All of us are saying, 'Hey, United States, we don't think this is a very good idea.'"

– King Abdullah II of Jordan, July 2002

Before the United States invaded Iraq, the great concern among its friends and dependents in the Arab world was that the resulting images of Americans shooting Arabs, Americans arresting Arabs, Americans *ruling* Arabs would have disastrous results in their own kingdoms and republics, where many people were already angry about the pro-American policies of their rulers. But it was seen at this point as a purely in-house Sunni peril: virtually every regime in the Arab world faces some sort of (Sunni) Islamist opposition movement, and the perceived danger was that the U.S. invasion of Iraq would drive people into the arms of those movements. What Osama bin Laden had envisaged as the result of an American invasion of Afghanistan was exactly what the rulers of the Arab countries feared as a result of the U.S. invasion of Iraq: everybody was on the same page. But now some of the leaders seem to have lost the plot: they are talking about the perils of a "Shia crescent" instead. (The actual phrase seems to be Abdullah's.)

"Most of the Shi'ites are loyal to Iran and not to the countries they are living in."

— Egyptian president Hosni Mubarak, 2006

Poor old Mubarak had to retract his comment, claiming that he had been talking only about the religious loyalties of Shias, not their national loyalties, after a storm of protest broke all across the Arab world, but he really did mean it. Fear of Shia "expansion" has become the flavour of the moment in the Sunni Arab world, and the beleaguered Sunni Arabs of Iraq play on it shamelessly. Even leaders of countries with no significant Shia minority of their own, like King Abdullah II of Jordan, have taken up the refrain: as early as 2005, he was warning that Iran's "vested interest" was "to have an Islamic [Shia] republic of Iraq. If that happened, we've opened ourselves to a whole new set of problems that won't be limited to the borders of Iraq."

Once again there was an outcry, with Lebanese journalist Joseph Samahah, editor of the Beirut newspaper *al-Akhbar* until his death in early 2007, leading the pack: "This is the first time an Arab official has used such crude, direct and dangerous language to publicly incite against a particular confession and warn that it may turn into a fifth column to be used against the minority." But it's not just crude and dangerous; it simply doesn't make sense.

Except for Iraq and Bahrain, both of which are about 60 per cent Shia, there are no Arabic-speaking countries with a Shia majority. Indeed, only three other Arab countries are more than 10 per cent Shia: Yemen, which is so far removed from the heart of the Arab world and so distinctive in its political culture that it would be misleading to include it in this discussion; Kuwait, where almost a third of the country's million citizens are Shias; and Lebanon, in the very heart of the Arab world, where Shias are politically self-conscious, highly organized, and would probably turn out to be about 35 to

40 per cent of the population if the government ever dared to take a census.

Shias in most Arab countries occupy the lower rungs of the socio-economic ladder, but it would be going too far to call them an oppressed minority. There have always been Sunni preachers who condemned Shias as heretics or infidels (and vice versa), but close personal, political, and commercial relations between Sunnis and Shias are commonplace wherever both sects are present in the Arab world. So how have Shias become a "fifth column" all of a sudden? How *could* they represent a serious threat to the established order in the Arab world, given their numbers and their relative poverty?

They don't. In Iraq, thanks to the American invasion, they have come to power quite democratically. With the exception of distant and isolated Yemen, where Zaydi (Shia) imams ruled the state until 1962, Iraq is the first Shia-ruled state in the Arab world since the fall of the Fatimid dynasty in Egypt more than eight hundred years ago. Perhaps that accounts for the sudden, shocked obsession with the Shia "threat": a Shia-ruled Iraq is as great an upheaval in the established order of things in the Arab world as a Brazil dominated by U.S.-style Protestant evangelicals would be to Latin Americans. (Just wait thirty years . . .) Its only concrete impact so far in the rest of the Arab world has been the arrival in Syria and Jordan each of upwards of a million refugees from Iraq, but in the psychological sense it has a far larger significance. Iraq, for many centuries a Sunni-ruled bulwark against the power of Shia Persia, has become instead (at least in the minds of many Arabs) the first foothold of expanding Iranian power in the Arab world.

The line where the Persian mountains meet the Mesopotamian plain has been a border between rival empires and a recurrent theatre of war for most of the past four thousand years. Iran, a single state that contains almost as many people as the whole of the eastern Arab world put together, still casts a giant shadow over the Fertile Crescent and the Arabian peninsula, and ever since the Persian empire became Shia under the Safavid dynasty in the early sixteenth century there has been a religious dimension to the chronic hostility as well. (Sunni insurgents in Iraq today commonly refer to their Shia fellow-countrymen as "safawi" – Safavid – and it is not a compliment.)

But there has *not* been an Iranian conquest of Iraq. There is Shia solidarity aplenty between Baghdad and Tehran nowadays, of course, but there are no Iranian troops in Iraq, nor are there likely to be. The Shias of Iraq do not need Iranian military help to maintain their control of central and southern Iraq, including most of Baghdad, and it is unlikely that an Iraqi government dominated by them would be subservient to Tehran. Most Shias in Iraq remain both Arab and specifically Iraqi in their orientations, as the huge influence of Moqtada al-Sadr clearly demonstrates.

It is almost unimaginable that any government in Baghdad would ask for Iranian troops to help in the task of suppressing the Sunni resistance in western Iraq, or that Tehran would agree to such a request. (There might be Iranian troops in Iraqi Kurdistan at some point, if the Kurds play their hand very badly, but that is not a region of immediate consequence for Iraq's Arab neighbours.) The notion of an Iranian military threat to the Arab world belongs in the realm of fantasy.

The regional balance of power has shifted and Iran has much more weight than it used to, but this does not mean that Iranian armoured divisions will soon be racing across the Fertile Crescent and seizing the oil fields on the Arab side of the Gulf. For one thing, Iranian armoured divisions do not race; they move at an arthritic crawl, and after the first few hundred kilometres or so their logistical support breaks down entirely. For another, why would Iran want to rule some tens of millions of rebellious Arabs and a bunch of burning oil fields? The United States has just given the Iranians a very convincing and entirely free demonstration of why trying to rule Arab states through a foreign military occupation is a really bad idea.

With a blithe disregard of the fact that it was the actions of the United States that created the alleged Iranian/Shia "threat" to the Arab world, American diplomacy is now trying to use the threat as a motivator for building some sort of alliance among what we would, by that logic, have to call the "front-line Arab states": Saudi Arabia and the smaller Gulf states, Jordan, and perhaps even Syria and Lebanon. "Containment" is an ever-popular notion among those who think the world is still a linear place where "front lines" mean something, but Washington is not having much success with this stratagem. Both Qatar, home to 6,500 American soldiers and the head-quarters for all U.S. air operations in the Middle East, and the United Arab Emirates, where there are about 1,300 U.S. troops, declared in March 2007 that they would not allow their territory to be used for a U.S. attack on Iran.

In the same month the Gulf Cooperation Council, a consultative group that joins those two states and four others, Kuwait, Saudi Arabia, Bahrain, and Oman, called on all of its members to do the same, which would make very good sense from their point of view. Saudi Arabia's Shia minority, although it probably accounts for only 10 per cent of the population, is heavily concentrated in the Eastern province along the country's Gulf coast (where all the oil is), where it makes up about half the population, and Riyadh has as little desire as Bahrain to put their loyalty to the test by getting into a war with Iran. All six Arab Gulf states are also within easy reach of Iranian missiles carrying conventional high-explosive warheads, and all would see their oil exports interrupted for an indefinite period of time if an American attack caused Iran to close the Gulf to shipping, so their enthusiasm for this course of action is understandably limited.

In the non-disaster scenario, where the United States does not attack Iran, there are no Arab countries where the alleged threat of a "Shia fifth column" is really relevant. Iraq, of course, is long past that "threat"; for better or for worse, it is a Shia-majority society ruled by a Shia-majority government. And the only other two Arab countries with really large Shia populations are Bahrain and Lebanon.

Tiny Bahrain has always had a Shia majority, and was at one time ruled by Iran. Like most of the smaller Arab kingdoms in the Gulf, it has a large foreign population, but two-thirds of its seven hundred thousand people are Arabs, and 60 per cent of the Arabs are Shias. Bahraini Shias inspired by the ideas of the Iranian revolution launched an unsuccessful coup attempt in 1981, and there was a lengthy period of rioting by Shia fundamentalists in the mid-1990s, triggered originally by women's participation in a sporting event: about forty people were killed. But in 1999 the new king, Sheikh Hamad bin Isa al-Khalifa, instituted elections for parliament, gave women the vote, and freed all political prisoners, since when politics in Bahrain has become a much more reasonable activity.

One should not get carried away with the vision of a democratic Bahrain. Both the largest Shia party and its main Sunni rival are conservative Islamic parties that vie for support by proposing "morality" measures like banning sorcery or the hanging of underwear on washing lines, and the forty-member elected lower house of parliament is balanced by an upper house appointed by Sheikh Hamad. In 2006, the main Shia party, Al-Wafaq National Islamic Society, won sixteen of the forty seats in an election where most people voted along sectarian lines, and it would be an exaggeration to say that Bahraini society is united even on basic values. But there is a mechanism for non-violent political change that may be sufficient to allow the Shia majority to realize its aspirations without any major upheavals, and most Bahrainis understand that their considerable prosperity (which is based much more on banking and other services than on oil) depends on maintaining an image of stability. Even a Shia-dominated government in Bahrain (presumably still under the King) would be very careful not to offend Sunni Arab sensibilities, especially since the island is connected to Saudi Arabia by a causeway, but it probably would request an early closure of the U.S. Navy's base in Bahrain.

So much for Shia-majority countries in the Arab world. The case of Lebanon is much more dramatic, even though Shias make up only 35 to 40 per cent of the population there. (No census has been held in Lebanon since 1932, mainly because a new census would compel the other Lebanese groups to acknowledge the relatively faster growth of the Shia population and redistribute the division of political power among the various confessional groups accordingly.) But the dominant Shia party in Lebanon, Hezbollah, is a military as well as a political organization, and a very competent one too. It fought for two decades against the Israeli occupation of south Lebanon (where most Lebanese Shias live), and inflicted so many casualties on the Israelis over the years that they eventually withdrew behind their own frontier in 2000. It fought the Israeli army to a standstill again during the war of July 2006, and its close links with Syria and Iran ensure that it does not lack for either money or weapons. As for the notion, much canvassed at the end of the 2006 war, that either the ten thousand UN troops now stationed in south Lebanon or the Lebanese army itself are going to "disarm" Hezbollah, it is simply laughable. Around 70 per cent of the Lebanese army's troops are Shia (because they are the poorest community in Lebanon – it's the usual story), so the army is certainly not going to take Hezbollah on. The mostly European UN troops didn't sign up for a war with Hezbollah either.

Quite apart from its own domestic divisions, Lebanon is cursed by having Israel to the south of it – and Syria, a neighbour with four times Lebanon's population, to the east. The regime in Damascus has never fully relinquished its claim to all of Lebanon, which was carved out of the old Ottoman province of Syria by the French colonialists in 1926 because the large Christian minority in Lebanon was relatively loyal to France, giving it a firmer grip on the Levantine coast. The Syrian regime is also interested in Lebanon for strategic reasons, because Syria has remained officially at war with Israel long after Egypt and Jordan made peace: unlike those two countries, it has never been able to make a deal with Israel that returned all of its conquered territory. For the past forty years, Israeli tanks on the occupied Golan Heights, formerly Syrian territory, have been only seventy-five kilometres from Damascus, so, from Syria's perspective, it would help greatly to restore the strategic balance if Syria could keep an army in Lebanon, relatively close to densely populated parts of Israel proper. It was the Lebanese civil war of 1975–90 that gave Damascus its chance.

In 1976, the Syrian regime got pan-Arab support to send Syrian "peace-keeping troops" into Lebanon, and they just forgot to go home again after the civil war ended in 1990. For thirty years Damascus manipulated Lebanese politics to ensure that there was no demand for their withdrawal, effectively paralyzing Lebanese democracy in the process, and the Shia party, Hezbollah, eventually became Syria's main local ally in this game.

Damascus valued Hezbollah highly because it was a huge nuisance to Israel, and Hezbollah used its Syrian alliance to advance the cause of the underprivileged Shia minority in Lebanon. But the assassination of former Lebanese prime minister Rafik Hariri in February 2005 upset that long, uneasy balance.

It was universally assumed in Lebanon that Hariri's killing had been organized by Syrian intelligence because he opposed the presence of Syrian troops in Lebanon, and the resulting mobilization of Sunni, Druze, and Christian opinion against Syria – most vividly expressed in the peaceful mass protests in Beirut that the Bush administration dubbed "the cedar revolution" – led to the full withdrawal of the Syrian army from Lebanon. In the election of May 2005, the freest in decades, the Lebanese elected a parliament in which Sunnis, Druze, and most Christians supported a Lebanon free from Syrian control and (implicitly) at peace with Israel – but the Shias, under-represented by the voting system and still out-siders in the Lebanese political game, overwhelmingly supported the Syrian connection and confrontation with Israel. The Syrian withdrawal might nevertheless have been a turning point in Lebanon's miserable history of communal strife punctuated by Israeli attacks if the Israelis had left the country alone for a while, but that was never likely. Instead, the country lost a decade's worth of reconstruction to massive Israeli air strikes in 2006, and was brought back to the brink of civil war.

It was, in one sense, the fault of the Shias, because it was their militia, Hezbollah, which made the attack on Israeli forces that provided the pretext for the Israeli onslaught. But the 2006 war was scheduled long in advance by Israel, with the approval of the United States, and the Israelis were just waiting for some provocation that would let them launch an all-out attempt to destroy Hezbollah.

"We told Israel, 'Look, if you guys have to go, we're behind you all the way. But we think it should be sooner rather than later.'

"The longer you wait, the less time we have to evaluate and plan for Iran before Bush gets out of office."
– A former U.S. intelligence officer, quoted in Seymour Hersh's article "Watching Lebanon," *The New Yorker*, August 21, 2006

Seymour Hersh probably has the best connections of any investigative journalist in the United States working on international affairs: from his first big story, the revelation of the My Lai massacre in Vietnam in 1969, down to U.S. policy in the Middle East today, he sets the industry standard for insider gossip. If you work for the American government and you want to spill the beans on something that you really disagree with, you call Hersh. His account of the long pre-planning for the Israeli attack on Hezbollah's positions in southern Lebanon is entirely plausible – "The Israelis told us it would be a cheap war with many benefits," an unidentified U.S. government consultant with close ties to the Israelis told Hersh.

"Why oppose it? We'll be able to hunt down and bomb missiles, tunnels and bunkers from the air. It would be a demo for Iran." Israeli prime minister Ehud Olmert later admitted as much to the Winograd Commission of Inquiry into the Israeli government's actions during the war, and further details emerged in a report in the *San Francisco Chronicle*.

"More than a year ago," the *Chronicle* reported on July 21, 2006, "a senior Israeli army officer began giving PowerPoint presentations, on an off-the-record basis, to U.S. and other diplomats, journalists and think-tanks, setting out the plans for the current operation in revealing detail." The details included a prediction that the war would last for three weeks, consisting mostly of aerial attacks but culminating in a ground invasion. Gerald Steinberg, professor of political science at Bar-Ilan University in Ramat Gan, told the *Chronicle* that "of all Israel's wars since 1948, this was the one for which Israel was most prepared. . . . By 2004, the military campaign scheduled to last about three weeks that we're seeing now had already been blocked out and, in the last year or two, it's been simulated and rehearsed across the board."

In reality, the war did not work out quite as Israel planned. Many or even most of Hezbollah's tunnels and bunkers near the Israeli border survived the Israeli bombing campaign (although much of Shia-majority southern Beirut was destroyed), Hezbollah rockets continued to fall on northern Israeli cities throughout the whole campaign, and Israel quickly abandoned the final phase of the operation, the land invasion, after taking heavy casualties from the dug-in Hezbollah fighters who had lived through the bombing. Both Ehud Olmert, who ordered the campaign, and the generals who waged it have been severely criticized in Israel, because the war was supposed to have re-established traditional Israeli "deterrence" – that is, the certain knowledge that any Arab attack on Israel would be punished a hundredfold – but had ended up confirming the opposite. Almost 1,000 Lebanese civilians and 33 Israeli civilians were killed, which is close to the traditional casualty exchange rate, but 119 Israeli soldiers were killed in ground combat against Hezbollah, which may have lost fewer than 300 fighters in return. That is *not* an exchange rate that Israelis are comfortable with.

The point of revisiting this horrific and futile episode is not to pin the blame for it on Israel, which is just another player in the game, no more or less ruthless than the others. It was Hezbollah that launched the attack across the Israeli frontier to kidnap Israeli soldiers on July 12, 2006, presumably with the aim of trading them for fifteen prisoners of war that Israel had taken during its occupation of Lebanon and failed to release when it withdrew. It was also Hezbollah that launched the first missiles across the frontier as a diversionary tactic during that operation. Similar incidents had occurred along the border on half a dozen occasions since the Israeli withdrawal from Lebanon in 2002, sometimes initiated by the Israelis, sometimes by Hezbollah, without causing a major escalation on Israel's part.

Hezbollah presumably calculated that this would just be another incident, and unwittingly provided the pretext – two Israeli soldiers kidnapped, and eight others killed on the same day, either in the initial attack or in a failed attempt to rescue the captives – for a long-planned Israeli offensive. So massive Israeli air raids were launched not only against Hezbollah positions in southern Lebanon but against Shia districts of Beirut and infrastructure targets throughout the country, and Hezbollah responded with a daily shower of (not very effective) missiles against cities and towns across northern Israel. The televised images of a military giant like Israel systematically smashing the virtually undefended hinterland of Lebanon from the air with complete impunity were so disturbing that international pressure for a ceasefire grew quickly, but the United States and Britain managed to stall the diplomatic process for three weeks in order to give their Israeli ally the time that had been allocated for the operation in the original plan.

By the end of the war, after the Israeli land invasion of southern Lebanon had been fought to a standstill and a UN–brokered ceasefire went into effect on August 14, 2006, large parts of Lebanon's physical infrastructure were destroyed, a considerable part of south Beirut was literally flattened, and the country had been brought back to the brink of civil war. It was, to say the least, inconsiderate on the part of Hezbollah to bring Israeli vengeance down on all of Lebanon – but none of this happened because the people in southern Lebanon were Shia.

The Shias of southern Lebanon live on the front line with Israel, and they have been thoroughly radicalized by the experience. (It is now usually forgotten that Shia villagers in the south were so alienated from the Lebanese state that they initially welcomed the Israeli invaders in 1982.) However, there isn't actually anything particularly "Shia" about their politics or their behaviour: if the dominant population in southern Lebanon at that time had been Sunni Arabs, they would have undergone a similar radicalization. It is Lebanon's bizarre "confessional" system of government that defines most of the people in the south as Shias, just as it defines others as Maronite Christians or Sunnis or Druze, and compels everybody to seek their goals and fight their battles within that sectarian framework. In recent years, some safer and more prosperous people in the centre and north of the country have been trying to break out of the confessional straitjacket and create a real Lebanese democracy, which would be a really good idea, but the Shias are trapped by both their geography and their poverty. They are armed and organized to fight not because they are Shias, but because they are people who wound up under Israeli military occupation and had to find their allies wherever they could.

And that's it for the Shia threat in the Arab world. All politics is local, and there is no "Shia crescent." Indeed, the regime that is most in danger because of the upheavals in Iraq is that of Syria itself, which is the closest thing to a Shia regime that the Arab world had to offer until recent events in Iraq.

To be fair, the ruling Ba'ath Party in Syria is formally a secular and inclusive body that makes no distinctions of ethnic or religious ties among Syrians and demands only obedience and at least lip service to Syria's Arab identity. In fact, however, Syria is as tightly controlled by a small group of closely related families as the Baathist regime in Iraq was, but with an important distinction. The families from Tikrit that controlled the Ba'ath Party in Iraq from the early 1970s, and that finally ended up as Saddam Hussein's indispensable inner circle, were indistinguishable in sect or ethnicity from other members of the traditional Sunni Arab ruling group. They just happened to know and trust one another, which gave them the jump on practically everybody else involved in Ba'ath Party politics in Iraq and ultimately brought them to the top. (Most politics in the Arab world is *very* local.) But the group of families that rules Syria is much more exotic.

They are Alawis, members of a sect so divergent in its beliefs and practices that even mainstream Shias generally regard them as heretics, although they clearly descend from the Shia tradition. Most of the 2-million-strong Alawi community (about a tenth of Syria's population) are simple farmers living in northwestern Syria, around the city of Latakia; however, a significant number of their sons were recruited into the army of the French colonial rulers of Syria, who preferred not to put military power into the hands of the orthodox Sunni Muslims who account for 75 per cent of Syria's population of 17.8 million. Once the French went home after the Second World War, the Alawi officers came into their own – as Arab nationalists, Syrian patriots, and Ba'ath Party members, of course, but also as members of a secretive sect and what amounted to a secret society.

With the 1970 coup of air force general Hafiz al-Assad, a former fighter pilot, the Alawis effectively came to power in Syria, for Assad was both Alawi and Baathist. Even more than the Tikritis did in Iraq, the Alawis in Syria have been meticulous in ensuring that other powerful groups in Syria get at least a moderately satisfactory share of the pie, but really important areas like the intelligence services are dominated by Alawis. Their control of the domestic situation is so comprehensive that the original Alawi dictator's death in 2000 (after a mere thirty years in office) caused scarcely a political ripple. Hafiz al-Assad's younger son Bashar, an ophthalmologist, succeeded to the presidency with no visible opposition (his elder brother Basil, who was originally groomed for the role, having wiped himself out in a James Dean–style car accident in 1994).

"[Bashar al-Assad] is the least worst dictator in the Arab world."
— A Syrian intellectual (who wishes to remain anonymous)

"The real opposition is the majority of the Syrian people. But they are afraid to speak out, and they have no rights. They live in a sea of fear."
– Another Syrian intellectual, who spent a long time in prison.
(Both interviewed by Paul Koring of
The Globe and Mail in May 2005)

Syria, in the phrase that Kanan Makiya used as the title of his 1989 book on Iraq under Saddam, is another "republic of fear." The fear is less intense, because neither Hafiz al-Assad nor his son have murdered and tortured suspected opponents of the regime in the psychopathic style of Saddam Hussein. They have killed and tortured when they thought it was necessary to stay in power, but they are no more brutal than they believe they have to be. Political prisoners may rot in jail for decades, but their families and tribes are not abused. Mobile phones, the Internet, and satellite television are freely available, but free speech about Syria is not permitted. It is in many ways like a late-period Communist regime in Eastern Europe (which is, after all, the Baathist model), where the population must still be silent and obedient, but ignorance and enthusiasm are no longer required. That was not a sustainable model in Europe, and it probably isn't in Syria either.

Bashar al-Assad has now been in power for seven years, and early hopes that he might be a radical reformer who would undo the Baathist dictatorship have been comprehensively dashed. He is in his person a modern man: he was once the head of the computer society in Damascus, and he married a Sunni Syrian woman whom he met when he was studying in London. But the hopes that this single person might transform the structures of power in Syria were never realistic, for he is essentially the instrument through which the Alawi clans hold power. Assad can try to reform the economy in modest ways, so long as he does not harm powerful vested interests, and he can make cosmetic reforms that allow public debate on issues that do not bring the regime's right to rule into question, but the fundamental problem is that political power in Syria is monopolized by a distinctive and widely distrusted religious minority. If the Alawis should ever lose power, after almost four decades of making decisions and enemies, it could be a night of many long knives.

"The Sunni Salafist movement with its jihadist offshoots is a growing force within Syria, especially among the rural young. This movement is not under the influence of traditional Islamist parties like the Muslim Brotherhood. It is a relatively new phenomenon, greatly boosted by the Iraq insurgency . . . it represents the strongest challenge to the regime on the ground."
 – Malik al-Abdeh, spokesman for the exiled (Syrian) Movement for Justice and Development, *The Guardian*, October 25, 2005

There are a few liberal, reformist Syrian exile parties that would not be out of place in a Western democracy, embodying the hopes of a generation of secular Syrian intellectuals now nearing pensionable age, but those parties have virtually no support in the Syrian street. Still much more important, despite the terrible beating it has taken over the years at the hands of the Syrian secret police, is the Muslim Brotherhood, a Sunni revolutionary movement which was once the principal threat to the Baathist regime. In 1979, it began a campaign of assassination against Baathists in general and Alawis in particular, often murdering not only officials but their entire families. In 1982, the Muslim Brotherhood launched a popular uprising in the cities of Aleppo and Hama, attacking army units stationed in the two cities and slaughtering the local Baathists. The regime regained control of Aleppo relatively easily, but in Hama it ended up smashing about half of the old city to rubble with tank and artillery fire. Then the Special Forces and Baathist security men conducted a block-by-block search in which the wounded and any other survivors who could not quickly and convincingly account for their presence were executed on the spot: the BBC estimated that twenty thousand died. It was a Syrian Fallujah – "shoot 'em all, and let God sort 'em out" – but the people who ordered it and those who carried it out were not foreigners but Syrians. The Syrian Ba'ath Party has less blood on its hands than its Iraqi rival did, but people who threaten its rule have a habit of dying violently.

Membership in the Muslim Brotherhood is still punishable by death in Syria, because it used to represent that kind of threat – but it is striking that the regime does not often invoke that penalty any more. It no longer judges the danger from the Muslim Brotherhood to be all that serious: the exiled leadership is out of touch, and even the surviving local members are greying rapidly. Now a bigger threat is young Islamist extremists imbued with the same Salafist doctrines that motivate al-Qaeda, radical, intolerant young men with such a strong faith in the purifying and clarifying power of violence that they would make a nineteenth-century European anarchist green with envy. (This is hardly a coincidence, as Osama bin Laden's version of Salafism is basically a shotgun marriage between millenary religious radicalism, not unknown even in the Sunni tradition, and secular European revolutionary extremism. Like the Jacobins, the extreme Islamists believe that terror can change entire societies.)

The exploits of the Sunni resistance in Iraq, and especially of the Islamist extremists among them, are having a huge impact on the poorly educated, frequently unemployed Sunni young of Syria (where 80 per cent of the population is under thirty-five). Just across the border in Iraq, other Arabs not very different from them have fought the U.S. Army to a standstill – and it is not lost on them that a lot of the people the Iraqi resistance kills are Shias, not all that different from the Alawi regime that has ruled Syria since long before they were born. Every day, moreover, another thousand or so Iraqi refugees slip across the border into Syria: most of them are Sunnis, and a significant proportion of them are Salafists. The homegrown revolutionary threat in Syria is nourished by unemployment of at least 20 per cent, a police state, and a per capita income of $1,040 (only one-fifth of South Africa's), but it is now being massively reinforced by events in the region.

There is another threat to Syria's stability ("stagnation" might be a better word): the emergence of an active and confident nationalist movement among the Kurdish minority of the northeast, inspired and fuelled to a large extent by the rise of Kurdish separatism in Iraq. Of the three discernible currents of opposition to the Syrian regime – the secular intelligentsia, the Islamists old and new, and the Kurdish nationalists – the Kurds probably presented the most acute danger to the Baathist regime during the first few years after the U.S. invasion of Iraq, because they were a potential fifth column that was ready to co-operate with any American plan for removing Assad from power in return for the same semi-independent status as their Iraqi Kurdish brothers. At that point, when Syria was an honorary fourth member of the "axis of evil," this was a plausible scenario, but the likelihood of an

American intervention to overthrow the status quo in Syria has dwindled drastically in the past year or two. Even the remaining neo-conservatives in the Bush administration have reluctantly concluded that U.S. interests are better served by the devil they know in Syria than by an upheaval that might bring Islamists to power there.

If the Ba'ath's grip on power in Damascus should weaken, the Kurds of Syria will certainly be a major player in the struggle for the country's future, but the United States has no current intention of overthrowing the Alawi regime. For Syria, the real threat to the existing order is neither Kurds nor Shias, but Islamist revolutionaries within the majority Sunni community. Like Saddam Hussein in his last decade, the Syrian Baathists are already trying to look more Islamic in an attempt to deflect the threat: Bashar al-Assad has taken to praying for the cameras, something that would once have been unthinkable in a secular Baathist republic, and a couple of years ago the sale of alcohol was banned in Aleppo, Syria's second city. The Ba'ath Party of Syria now regularly warns that if it is overthrown, its successor will be an Islamic republic, and that is probably true not just for Syria, but for any other Sunni Arab state that experiences a revolution in the next ten years.

"All over the Arab world, the Islamists have the majority in the street."
– Azzam al-Huneidi, leader of the Islamic bloc,
Jordanian parliament, quoted in *The Boston Globe*, March 21, 2006

In Jordan, there is theoretically no need of a revolution, because there have been regular parliamentary elections for a long time. In practice, the elections are strictly controlled, with all candidates obliged to run as independents (no party affiliations to be mentioned) and heavily gerrymandered electoral districts. But there is a powerful Islamic movement, linked to the Muslim Brotherhood in Egypt and Hamas in the Israeli-occupied territories, and its Islamic Action Party (IAP) regularly wins about 15 per cent of the seats in parliament. It received an enormous boost from the electoral victory of Hamas in the Palestinian territories in January 2006, for a majority of Jordan's 5 million people are actually Palestinians by descent, and leading IAP members recently claimed that in a fully free election the Islamic Action Party would win 40 to 50 per cent of the seats. That may be why there has been some talk about postponing the next parliamentary elections for a while.

The basic problem with Jordan is that it is mainly just lines on a map, representing no particular historical or tribal reality. The ruling Hashemite dynasty hails from the Hejaz, now part of Saudi Arabia, and was instrumental in inciting the Arab revolt against the Turks during the First World War: the founder of the dynasty was recruited to the British cause by Lawrence of Arabia. The British gave the Hashemites the throne of "Transjordan," as the kingdom was called at first, after the Saudis conquered the Hejaz in 1924, and they brought many supporters with them, but there has always been an artificiality about the state. The core support for the regime comes from the Bedouin tribes, many of them originally from the Hejaz, and the army in particular retains a strongly Bedouin character, but successive waves of refugees out of Palestine over the years mean that the kingdom's population is now up to 70 per cent Palestinian. (As in Lebanon, census data are unavailable or unbelievable.) Jordan made peace with Israel in 1994, but the deal has never been popular with the public.

There have been repeated bouts of instability in the country when the dynasty's instinctively pro-Western orientation clashes too sharply with the emotional loyalties of the bulk of the population, most notably during the "Black September" crisis of 1970, which ended with the Jordanian army driving the Palestine Liberation Organization out of the country. But the PLK – "plucky little king," as King Hussein (1953–2002) was known to generations of journalists – was a born survivor, and knew just when to defer to his subjects on emotionally important subjects. It is not clear that his son, King Abdullah II, has the same adroitness, and he has noticeably tightened the repression since he came to the throne, but the presumption remains that Jordan will not spin out even if the Islamic Action Party somehow wins a parliamentary majority, precisely because there is a democratic system of sorts. The Islamic parties have never made a repudiation of the peace treaty with Israel a formal part of their program, although they have never endorsed it either. Jordan, despite its extreme fragility (now exacerbated by the presence of so many Iraqi refugees), is not a leading candidate for an Islamist revolution.

"The Muslim Brotherhood committed 9/11 through its offshoots. All of them, Islamic Jihad, Hamas, Gemal Islamiya, are offshoots of the Muslim Brotherhood. There is no such thing as a moderate Islamist."
– Ahmed Aboul Gheit, Egyptian foreign minister,
The Independent, June 21, 2005

The Muslim Brotherhood, even in its relatively tame Egyptian version, shares many theological, philosophical, and political positions with Palestinian Islamist groups like Hamas and Islamic Jihad that wage an armed struggle against Israel, and even with international terrorist groups like al-Qaeda, but they occupy very different points along the same spectrum. Seeking to exclude all Islamist groups from politics on the pretext that they are all equally dangerous to democracy, or even banning democracy itself (as happens in many Arab states) on the pretext that it would give the Islamists a chance of gaining power, are ultimately self-defeating strategies because they excuse the Islamists from ever having to deal with the realities of power in an intractable world. In Syria, in Jordan, in Egypt, even in Saudi Arabia, Islamists enjoy the luxury of being critics exempt from ever having to show how they themselves would deal with the country's problems, and the moral superiority of being victims of state repression. The long-term solution – forgive me for sounding like a neo-con here – is more democracy, not less, even though most people in the West would be alarmed by the initial results.

Begin with a proposition that seems to me self-evident, and that would have saved the United States much waste of blood and money if the neo-conservatives had grasped it five years ago: democracy does not automatically make people like U.S. foreign policy. To anyone with even a glancing knowledge of the Arab world, it has long been obvious that the first result of a democratic election in almost any Arab country would be a government that took its distance from the United States, and that Washington would ultimately come to see as at least unreliable, if not an outright enemy.

One recent example of this is Iraq, although the transformation of the democratically elected government in Baghdad from a mere puppet to a deeply dependent ally and eventually onwards to a fully independent regime that opposes most U.S. policies in the Middle East is not yet complete.

Another, more obvious example is in the Palestinian occupied territories, where a fully democratic election in early 2006 gave Hamas, an Islamist party condemned by Israel, the United States, and most of its European allies as a terrorist organization, the right to form a government. Israel and the Western powers responded, of course, with embargoes, boycotts, and condemnations, for the Palestinians had failed to understand that some views are less acceptable than others in an Arab democracy, but the surprising thing is that the American and Israeli governments were actually surprised.

A revival of Islam as a political force has been underway ever since the 1970s, and it has made particularly deep inroads in the Arab countries. The leaders of this movement do see the West as the enemy and are intolerant of other Muslims who do not share their views and values, but none of that should come as news given the specific historical context of this movement and the generally intolerant nature of big religious revivals. When changes have been so great and so rapid that the whole society is effectively in shock, the most common response of people whose lives seemed to be beyond their control is to turn to religion – and, in particular, to fundamentalist forms of religion that promise a return to the old values and the old ways.

There are five or six times as many Arabs as there were a hundred years ago, and a society that was at least 90 per cent rural then is now well over half urban. Industrialization has largely failed, but there are many millions of ex-peasants in the cities who would have factory jobs if they had any jobs at all. City living and mass education (however scanty) have undermined the traditional hierarchies of age and gender. And to these domestic ills, you can add the foreign ones: the Arab countries were all conquered by European empires and ruled by foreigners and their local collaborators for a generation or more. They won their independence in the 1940s and 1950s only to discover that they were still poor, still oppressed, and still losing: six military defeats at the hands of Israel and its Western friends in the course of sixty years. Everything has gone wrong, and only a return to the old-time religion can put it right. Not the *real* old-time religion, of course, but a juiced-up, populist, extreme form of the religion that offers simple answers to the questions of the disoriented and the dispossessed. It is technically wrong to call the resulting religious movement Islamic fundamentalism, but it certainly shares the same social roots as Christian fundamentalism, and has the same certainty that there are religious answers to the secular problems brought on by over-rapid change.

It would be very surprising if the "Islamists" were still a dominant political phenomenon in the Arab world in 2100, or even in 2050. Historically, great religious revivals of this sort usually have a life cycle of one to two generations, and it's unlikely that this one will follow different rules. At the moment, however, the rise of Islamic and Islamist political movements has been the dominant reality of Arab politics almost everywhere for about thirty years, and the real anomaly is that this broad social and intellectual movement is so little reflected in the political and legal reality of Arab countries. If they had democratic systems, legitimate political parties would have adopted some of their ideas and put them into practice long ago. Some laws that secular people deeply dislike would have been passed, some politicians spouting what sounds like nonsense to secular people would have achieved positions of power for a while – and then after a few decades, as the excitement died down, normal political service would gradually have been restored.

It could not happen that way in the Arab world because there are few Arab countries with democratic political systems. In the absence of legitimate political parties that might adopt and promote their ideas, those who believed that the solution to the Arab world's problems was more Islam created their own (mostly illegal) political movements – and being illegal, naturally they were radicalized to some degree. That was thirty years ago, in most cases, but although their popular support has grown over the years, even now none of those parties is in power in the Arab world. To put them there would require revolutions, and the revolutions haven't happened. One consequence has been a further radicalization that has led, at the margin, to apocalyptic terrorist movements like al-Qaeda.

However, the remarkable success of the existing Arab regimes in excluding the Islamic parties from power for so long depended on a balance of forces that has been severely destabilized by recent events. The defeat of U.S. military power in Iraq by insurgents who are mainly Islamist in their beliefs has gravely undermined the implicit American guarantee to protect most existing Arab regimes, at the same time as it has enormously enhanced the prestige of Islamists everywhere. Moreover, it seems probable that western Iraq, for some time to come, will be a safe haven for Islamist extremists who want to overthrow other Arab regimes by violent revolutions. The likelihood of some sort of Islamic group or party coming to power sooner or later, by election or by revolution, has just got a lot bigger in most of the larger Arab countries.

That is the situation, and so the only relevant question is: Starting from here, what would be the least bad outcome? It would be a region in which most Arab countries from Egypt to Saudi Arabia have become much more democratic, and

Islamic parties understand that they have at least a fair chance of coming to power by electoral means (and some are actually in power). In such a "best available" scenario, no Arab countries would fall into the hands of the real crazies who want to recreate what they imagine were the conditions of seventh-century Arabia, and relations between the Arab world and the rest of the world, while even pricklier than now, would not be utterly poisonous. It is a measure of how desperate things have become that even these modest expectations already sound like wishful thinking.

The old regimes now face a fundamental choice. Do they start opening up some sort of democratic system, in the hope that modest moves in that direction could buy them some time and ensure that the eventual transition to democratically elected governments, even if they turn out to be Islamic in their orientations, will not be violent or vengeful? Or do they decide just to increase the repression, reckoning that *some* regimes, at least, are likely to survive? In terms of what would be better for the country as a whole, the right choice for almost any country in the Arab world would be the first: its people get democracy, and if they do decide they want an Islamic government, at least they are likely to choose a moderate one that understands economics and doesn't want war.

In terms of which is the better choice for any existing regime, however, the argument probably goes the other way, because if it goes with the first option it is putting itself out of business. The end may come gently, leaving the country a much better future, but the old regime will end, whereas if it digs in and resists all change, it just might pull through, at least for a good long while. Intransigence has a high potential cost, of course: if a regime does decide that it would rather die in the last ditch than relinquish power, it may end up doing just that, very messily, and the revolution that overthrows it will probably deliver the country into the hands of brutal fanatics like al-Qaeda or the Taliban. But barring a sudden outbreak of altruism in the existing Arab governments, few of them are likely to choose the path of compromise and hand over power peacefully.

The Muslim Brotherhood in Egypt is the oldest Islamist party of all. In the last parliamentary election in Egypt in 2005, which was rigged in a number of ways but less blatantly so than before, its members, running as "independents," managed to win about one-fifth of the seats in the Egyptian parliament, increasing its presence almost sixfold from fifteen to eighty-eight members. If there were genuinely free elections in Egypt, with six months' notice for formerly banned parties to organize and equal access to the mass media for all parties, the Muslim Brotherhood would probably end up as the Egyptian government. But the Egyptian regime has already opted for the last ditch.

The Egyptian constitution is now in the process of being modified by the Mubarak regime so that there are no more accidents like the 2005 election. In March 2007, the parliament in Cairo, still dominated by the regime's placemen, passed a series of constitutional amendments that strip away the right of Egyptian citizens to a trial before a judge if accused of "terrorism" (in future, it will be a military tribunal), that allow the government to search homes, bug phones, and read e-mails without a warrant, and that remove judicial supervision of elections (which was intended to prevent vote-rigging). It may fairly be said that these amendments, duly approved in a referendum with an alleged 80 per cent turnout (although there doesn't seem to be anybody at the polling stations), will make little difference in practice, as Egypt has been under "emergency rule," with most constitutional rights suspended since 1981. But they clearly show that the regime intends to resist change to the bitter end.

The same is true of Syria (where the charade of "elections" is even more transparently cynical than in Egypt, and emergency rule has been in force for forty-four years). It may or may not be true of Jordan, where the fact that two-thirds of the population is actually Palestinian confuses the issue, but Hamas would at least make a respectable showing if it were free to run in Jordan's (relatively honest) elections. And the Saudi Arabian regime has a special problem, for the Saudi ruling family bases its right to rule on its role as the upholder of Islamic values and the defender of the sacred places of Islam (Mecca and Medina) – but the holy places it acquired by conquest less than a century ago, and its claim to be the guardian of Islamic values derives from a deal done between the founder of the dynasty, Muhammad ibn Saud, and Muhammad ibn Abd al-Wahhab, a puritanical religious reformer, in 1744, back in the family's native region of Nejd. For more than two and a half centuries the alliance has held, with the Wahhabi religious establishment providing Islamic validation of the secular acts of the al-Saud family in return for a near-monopoly over official religious establishments in the country. (They even issued a fatwa authorizing the basing of infidel American troops in Arabia during the 1990–91 Gulf War.)

The burgeoning oil wealth of the past half-century has imposed huge strains on the devout and socially conservative population of Saudi Arabia. The wealth has brought unprecedented opportunities for immoral and corrupt behaviour, the population has quintupled in fifty years and continues to explode (more than half of Saudi Arabia's people are under fifteen), and the traditional, highly personal style of government has become less and less appropriate as the scale of the state has grown twenty- or thirty-fold. The al-Saud's family's major response to the new challenges, apart from creating a cradle-to-grave welfare state for its citizens, has been to emphasize its religious legitimacy, creating a new religious police force (the *mutawayyin*) to enforce public morals and building up the religious sector in higher education: by the 1990s, one-quarter of university students in Saudi Arabia were pursuing Islamic studies. But the surge in wealth and in education was bound to produce a more organized and articulate opposition to the family's absolute rule, and in the particular context of Saudi Arabia it was inevitable that most of the opposition would attack the regime from an Islamic standpoint.

There are those in Saudi Arabia who criticize the al-Saud family on secular grounds, highlighting the way that members of the family exploit their power for financial gain, but they are not a major factor in the political equation. The real opposition is all Islamic (or Islamist) in tone, but divided between those who demand reform – not necessarily Western-style democracy, but more effective consultation between the rulers and the ruled, an end to the flagrant corruption in royal and government circles, and above all adherence to the rule of law – and those who have given up on reform and advocate the violent overthrow of the monarchy: the jihadis. The latter are greatly outnumbered by the former, no doubt, but there are enough jihadis that the kingdom has had a significant terrorist problem for a long time.

The seizure of the Grand Mosque in Mecca by Islamist

extremists in 1979 shocked the kingdom to the core, particularly when it became clear that the leader, Juhaiman al-Utaibi, was a former captain in the Saudi Arabian National Guard, a force that recruits heavily in the Saudis' home region of Najd and serves as a kind of Praetorian Guard for the family. The same year saw a Shia uprising in the Eastern Province, inspired by the Iranian revolution across the Gulf, that ended with the bulldozing of the ancient downtown section of the city of Qatif. The two events caused a certain amount of panic in the regime, but there were no further attacks for more than a decade. The sustained jihadi assault only began following the decision to allow the permanent basing of American troops in Saudi Arabia after the first Gulf War, and opened with a 1996 attack on the al-Khobar towers in the Eastern Province that killed nineteen American servicemen. (The government blamed pro-Iranian Shias at the time, but it was almost certainly an al-Qaeda operation.)

The jihadis really went into high gear after the U.S. invasion of Iraq in March 2003, killing more than fifty people in two suicide attacks on foreigners' residential compounds in Riyadh in May and November. The attacks intensified in 2004, with a car-bomb at the former headquarters of General Security in Riyadh, an assault on a large petrochemical complex at Yanbu on the Red Sea coast, and an attack on a foreigners' residential compound in al-Khobar that left twenty-two dead. In December 2004 alone there was an attack on the U.S. consulate in Jeddah and car-bombs outside the Ministry of the Interior and a training facility of the Special Emergency Forces (an anti-terrorist SWAT team) in Riyadh.

Had the attacks continued at this pace, the foreigners who provide much of the kingdom's workforce would have begun to leave the kingdom in droves, but a wave of shoot-outs and arrests then thinned the terrorists' ranks (Saudi security forces claim to have killed 140 members of "al-Qaeda in the Arabian Peninsula" since May 2003) and the scale and frequency of the attacks fell sharply. Another wave of arrests followed in April 2007, with 172 people detained on charges of preparing suicide attacks on oil installations, public figures, and military bases in the kingdom and abroad. Some of them, claimed General Mansour al-Turki, security spokesman for the Interior Ministry, had been trained as pilots. The planning had reached an advanced stage, he said, and "what remained was only to set the zero hour for their attacks. They had the personnel, the money and the arms."

It's hard to know what to make of this kind of assertion, or indeed to judge how strong support is for the jihadi cause within Saudi Arabia. The extremists can obviously rely on some significant number of sympathizers, and the insurgency across the border in Iraq must be giving useful experience to many Saudi Arabian volunteers. On the other hand, the withdrawal of American troops from the kingdom has taken much internal pressure off the regime, and the higher oil prices of the last few years has ended its cash-flow problems and increased its ability to buy off dissident groups. If the Iraqi government fails to establish control over the "Sunni triangle" after the departure of the American forces, and that area becomes the much-touted "nest of terrorists" that we are encouraged to worry about, would that tip the internal balance in Saudi Arabia in favour of the jihadis?

It seems unlikely to do so, although it might well lead to a new upsurge in terrorist attacks in the kingdom. Frustration with the royal family is a common theme in Saudi Arabia, but it would be very hard to get rid of it: there are at least seven thousand princes, and they are involved in every significant enterprise and institution in the country. The al-Saud family marries into every tribe, every powerful merchant family, every influential clerical family, and they have been doing this for several centuries. The way that some of them use their influence for personal gain is often resented, but this is not a regime tottering on the brink of collapse. If you have to put your money down, you should probably bet on its survival.

Farther afield, the Algerian generals, who fought a bloody civil war against Islamist rebels after cancelling an election in 1991 that more moderate Islamic parties were winning, are most unlikely to let religious parties back into politics. Tunisia's ruling party allows only token opposition, and Libya's Colonel Muammar Gaddafi has no plans to give up supreme power after only thirty-eight years. Only relatively liberal Morocco has a parliamentary system that might allow Islamic parties to come to power peacefully (or peacefully fail to win the necessary votes). In most parts of the Arab world, the Islamists will have to fight for power. In some places, they will win, but nobody knows which ones.

"The real blame should be directed at us, the leaders of the Arab nation. Our constant disagreements and rejection of unity have made the Arab nation lose confidence in our sincerity and lose hope."
— King Abdullah of Saudi Arabia,
Arab League summit, March 28, 2007

There is one wild card that remains to be played, and the Arab regimes are feeling desperate enough to play it. At the Arab League summit meeting in Riyadh on March 28–29,

2007, they declared that the entire Arab world is still ready for peace with Israel if it withdraws from all the Arab lands that it seized in the 1967 war and agrees to a just solution to the plight of the Palestinian refugees who fled or were driven out of what is now Israel in 1948–49. If this deal could actually be made – a big *if* – would it forestall the political upheavals that otherwise seem very likely in the Arab world?

It is a measure of the concern felt by the established Arab regimes that in 2007 they essentially reissued an offer for a comprehensive peace settlement that they first made in 2002. At that time it was completely ignored by Israel, as Ariel Sharon was the Israeli prime minister and had no interest in trading land for peace, but it is nevertheless virtually unknown in the diplomatic world to make the same offer again at a later date – it looks too much like begging. Israel's pretext for rejecting the offer out of hand in 2002 was the Arab demand that Palestinian refugees and their descendants be allowed to return to their original homes within what is now Israel if they wished, which could seriously dilute the Jewish majority within Israel, as millions of them might theoretically choose to return. But that demand (which was also the deal-breaker in the Camp David talks between Palestinian leader Yasser Arafat and Israeli prime minister Ehud Barak in 2000) was probably negotiable even in 2002, and it certainly is now. If Israel now wants to make such a deal with the Arab League, it can probably have it, and not have to accept the return of more than a token number of refugees. The question now is whether the Israelis can be sure that the regimes it might make such a deal with will actually survive long enough to make it worthwhile.

"Israel could always do business with Arab dictators, a barrier protecting it from the rage of the 'Arab street.' That was the basis of the peace agreements with Egypt and Jordan, [and with] Yasser Arafat and his heirs, and [the basis of] the rules vis-à-vis Syria and Jordan. But those days are over. Henceforth Israel will have to factor into its foreign policy something it has always ignored – Arab public opinion."

– Aluf Benn, diplomatic editor of the
Israeli newspaper *Ha'aretz*, April 2006

Those regimes are making the offer because they believe, rightly or wrongly, that a real settlement with Israel that ended the long ordeal of the Palestinians would remove a huge irritant from the domestic politics of every Arab state and improve their chances of surviving, but they are unable to guarantee that they will survive. If they do not, then Israel would have made large concessions for a peace settlement that would collapse as the established Arab regimes fall. It is not just the Arab regimes that face an existential crisis. Israel does, too.

CHAPTER VIII

ISRAEL'S DILEMMA

Creveld: We've fought our external enemies for so many years. Each time there was a war, we took a mighty hammer to our foes, and after being defeated a few times, they left us alone. The problem with the Palestinian revolt is that it doesn't come from without, but rather from within. . . .

Interviewer: Is the solution, then, to keep the Palestinians outside the borders?

Creveld: Exactly, and right now there's nearly unanimous agreement on that. We ought to build a wall "so high, that not even a bird can fly over it." The only problem is: where to put the border? Since we can't decide whether the territories conquered in 1967 should be included, for the time being we improvise a little. . . .

Interviewer: Does that mean that the Palestinians stay within the borders?

Creveld: No, it means that they all get deported. The people who strive for this are waiting only for the right man and the right time. Two years ago only 7 or 8 per cent of Israelis were of the opinion that this would be the best solution, two months ago it was 33 per cent and now, according to a Gallup poll, the figure is 44 per cent.

Interviewer: Will that ever be possible?

Creveld: Sure, since desperate times give rise to desperate measures. Today there's a fifty-fifty split on where the border should run.

Two years ago 90 per cent wanted the wall built along the old border. That has completely changed now, and if things continue, if the terror doesn't stop, in another two years perhaps 90 per cent will want to build the wall along the Jordan [river]. The Palestinians talk of summutt, meaning hang tough, cling to the ground and the soil. I have enormous respect for the Palestinians. They fight heroically. But if we in fact want to strike across the Jordan, we would need only a few brigades. If the Syrians or the Egyptians were to try to stop us, we'd wipe them out. . . .

Interviewer: Do you think that the world will allow that kind of ethnic cleansing?

Creveld: That depends on who does it and how quickly it happens. We possess several hundred atomic warheads and rockets and can launch them at targets in all directions. . . . Most European capitals are targets for our air force.

Interviewer: Wouldn't Israel then become a rogue state?

Creveld: Let me quote General Moshe Dayan: "Israel must be like a mad dog, too dangerous to bother." I consider it all hopeless at this point. We shall have to try to prevent things from coming to that, if at all possible. Our armed forces, however, are not the thirtieth-strongest in the world, but rather the second or third. We have the capability to take the world down with us. And I can assure you that that will happen, before Israel goes under.

Interviewer: This isn't your own position, is it?

Creveld: Of course not. You asked me what might happen and I've laid it out. The only question is whether it is already too late for the other solution (the two-state solution), which I support, and whether Israeli public opinion can still be convinced. I think it's too late. With each passing day the expulsion of the Palestinians grows *more probable. The alternative would be the total annihilation and disintegration of Israel.*

What do you expect from us?

– Martin van Creveld, professor of military history, Hebrew University of Jerusalem, interview by Ferry Biedermann published in the Dutch magazine *Elsevier*, February 2003

M artin van Creveld is not just the leading military historian in Israel, he is the only non-American writer on war who is on the required reading list for U.S. Army officers. However, he is reviled by many in Israel for saying the things that nobody is supposed to say aloud, and this interview is a case in point. At the time, he was deeply concerned that then-prime minister Ariel Sharon would use the distraction provided by the forthcoming U.S. invasion of Iraq to carry out a high-speed ethnic cleansing of the occupied West Bank and Gaza Strip, driving the bulk of the Palestinian inhabitants across the old international frontiers of the United Nations Mandate of Palestine into Jordan and Egypt, and his comments about Israel's ability to deter outside intervention in support of the Palestinians by threatening nuclear strikes against European capitals were made in that context.

That time has now passed: Sharon is no longer prime minister, a wall that incorporates only a part of the West Bank into Israel is under construction, Israeli settlements have been withdrawn from the Gaza Strip, and terrorist attacks on Israel have dropped sharply. On the other hand, van Creveld's belief that the final disposition of the Palestinian question is of life-and-death importance to Israel continues to be shared by the majority of his fellow-countrymen, and only three stable outcomes are imaginable. There is the "two-state solution," with

Israeli and Palestinian states more or less defined by the pre-1967 borders living side by side in the territory of the former Palestine Mandate; this has been the preferred option of most moderates in both Israel and the Arab world for the past fifteen or twenty years, but now seems to be sliding out of reach. There is the "one-state solution," favoured by more radical Palestinians who rely on demography to ensure a Palestinian majority in that same territory in the long run, and propose that its future should be decided by free elections in which everybody living there, or with a right to return there – the one-tenth of Israel's Jewish citizens who actually live elsewhere, and the much larger number of Palestinian refugees and their descendants who live outside the occupied territories – has an equal vote on its political future. And there is the "transfer" solution, in which the Jewish character of Israel is preserved without relinquishing its broader post-1967 borders by "transferring" (i.e., expelling) most of the Palestinians who live within those borders. (There used to be a fourth possible outcome – "drive the Jews into the sea" – but that ceased to be an Arab option even before Israel became a major nuclear power.)

Van Creveld's discussion seems a bit dated at the moment, since the "transfer" option is less prominent in Israel today than it was in 2003, but it never goes away for good. I have included it anyway because it expresses some strategic realities that are normally buried beneath the sentimentality and moralizing that pass for analysis in much Western discussion of Middle Eastern questions. Israel is a state like any other, with no permanent friends but only permanent interests. It often has great internal difficulty in deciding precisely what those interests are, since basic questions about the state's borders and ethnic composition remain unsettled, but its willingness to use force or the threat of force to safeguard those interests – including nuclear force, if necessary – should not be in doubt. Nor is it only Arabs or Iranians who might at some point find that Israel's nuclear weapons capabilities have become a relevant consideration when they are deciding what to do next.

Israel is probably the world's fifth-largest nuclear power, with more nuclear warheads than Britain. It began acquiring Dolphin-class submarines from Germany in the late 1990s (the eventual planned total is five), and subsequently equipped them with cruise missiles (based on the U.S. "Harpoon" missile) that can deliver nuclear weapons to almost anywhere around the Mediterranean, the Red Sea, the Persian Gulf, or the Arabian Sea. Israel is unquestionably the greatest military power in the Middle East, and it has been decades since any Arab army seriously contemplated attacking it: if they ever did start to gain the advantage in a conventional war, they would immediately face Israeli nuclear weapons.

Yet Israel's position is still far from secure politically, for despite six decades of existence and a tenfold growth in population it has failed to gain acceptance from its Arab neighbours. In the twelfth century the Crusader states looked pretty secure sixty years after the conquest of Jerusalem, too, but the only real guarantee of the country's long-term survival is to become a recognized part of the regional state system and economy. That was always going to be very difficult for Israel to achieve, due to the nature of its foundation.

There is no moral distinction to be made between the creation of Israel and the creation of earlier European colonial societies like the United States, Canada, and Mexico – New England, New France, and New Spain, as parts of them were once known – but there are two major practical distinctions.

One is that the typical European "New World" colony (a term that embraces Australasia as well as the Americas) sought to dispossess a sparse hunter-gatherer population that was hopelessly vulnerable to Eurasian diseases and replace it with a European population. The diseases did most of the invaders' killing for them, and the few survivors of the original population were driven onto reservations. But the project got a great deal more challenging when there was a relatively dense native population with even an early form of civilization (as five centuries of bitter Mexican history and the faces of the present Mexican population attest), or when the European settlers did not have a whole battery of quick-killer epidemic diseases fighting on their side (which is the main reason that European settlers never managed to establish successful white-majority colonies anywhere on the shores of Asia or Africa).

"[The Palestinians] look upon Palestine with the same instinctive love and true fervor that any Aztec looked upon Mexico or any Sioux looked upon his prairie. Palestine will remain for the Palestinians not a borderland, but their birthplace, the center and basis of their own national existence."

– Ze'ev Jabotinsky in 1923.
Quoted in Benny Morris, *Righteous Victims*, 1999

Jabotinsky, the founder of the "Revisionist" school of Zionism and the intellectual godfather of Herut, Likud, and Kadima, the right-wing parties that have dominated Israeli politics for most of the past thirty years, is often vilified as a proto-fascist, but he was just a man of his time who had the courage to call a spade a spade. Born in Russia in 1880, he moved to Palestine after the First World War, and he consistently fought against those softer souls who wanted to believe in a peaceful Zionism, a Zionism without victims. "Zionism is a colonizing adventure," he insisted, "and, therefore, it stands or falls on the question of armed forces." However, the Zionists who dreamt of creating Israel in the late nineteenth and early twentieth centuries were defying all of the colonial rules, because the Palestinians weren't actually "natives" in the sense that the Sioux or even the Aztecs had been.

The Zionist project envisaged the creation of a new European colony in the midst of a large, long-established population on the shores of the eastern Mediterranean, an enterprise that was tried once and abandoned eight hundred years ago. Apart from more money, better weapons, and outside support, the settlers would have only marginal advantages over the resident Arab population, whose civilization was just as old and sophisticated as their own, even if it had lost much ground both technologically and politically in recent centuries. They had no demographic advantages, either: both the settlers and the natives had the same vulnerabilities to disease, and while European Jewish families were undoubtedly as big or bigger than Palestinian Arab families (if only because more of their children survived) at the time when the Zionists began dreaming their dream, they were unquestionably smaller by the time the state of Israel actually came into existence in 1948. The Zionist enterprise was, therefore, a very ambitious undertaking, to say the least.

The other great distinction between Israel and earlier European attempts to create colonies overseas was that by the time Israel came along, both the legal and the political environments were changing. The era of European domination of the world was drawing to a close, the empires were falling apart, and a new international majority of ex-colonial countries with large chips on their shoulders was taking the place of the tight group of European countries and white European ex-colonies that had made up almost the entire "international community" a quarter-century before.

At the same time, a new international legal framework was taking shape, principally around the institutions of the newly founded United Nations, which made genocide, ethnic cleansing, and other traditional colonial techniques for removing inconvenient indigenous populations illegal and criminal. (Israelis sometimes feel they are being judged by a double standard, since Americans, Argentines, and Australians did considerably worse things to their "natives" without condemnation in the past.)

Above all, Israel was created three years after the Charter of the United Nations declared that border changes through war were no longer acceptable. It got away with the very considerable expansion of the territory allotted to it under the original UN partition plan, ending up with four-fifths of Palestine rather than half, because the ceasefire line at the end of the 1948–49 war became the new international frontier. However, no subsequent acquisition of territory by force would be recognized by anybody, so Israel was legally stuck with the 1948 borders unless it could negotiate a change with its Arab neighbours, which didn't seem very likely. This was just one of a number of reasons why Israelis grew to dislike the United Nations. But however much they may resent the workings of international law, Israelis are also its beneficiaries: their legal existence as a sovereign state came to them by grace of a resolution of the United Nations. All they had to do then was make it Jewish – which involved removing most of the Arab population.

"We shall try to spirit the penniless [Arab] population across the border by procuring employment for it in the transit countries, while denying it employment in our own country. . . . The removal of the poor must be carried out discreetly and circumspectly."

– Theodor Herzl, the founder of the
Zionist World Organization, diary entry, 1895

"Jewish villages were built in the place of Arab villages. . . . Nahlal arose in the place of Mahlul; Kibbutz Gvat in the place of Jibta; Kibbutz Sarid in the place of Huneifis; and Kefar Yehushu'a in the place of Tal al-Shuman. There is not one single place built in this country that did not have a former Arab population."

– Moshe Dayan, minister of defence in the 1967 and 1973 wars;
address to Technion University students, Haifa,
reported in *Ha'aretz*, April 4, 1969

The question of "transfer" – of removing at least enough of the existing Arab population to ensure a Jewish majority in the planned state – was always an awkward issue for the Zionist leaders, most of whom salved their consciences by pretending (at least in public) that the Zionist project was simply a case of "a people without land returning to a land without people." No Jewish state would be possible in Palestine unless there was a mass displacement of its Arab inhabitants, who would otherwise constitute a huge fifth column in its midst, but there was no Zionist master-plan in 1948 for the expulsion of the Arab population from the parts of Palestine assigned to the Jewish state by the United Nations partition plan or subsequently conquered during the 1948–49 war. Transfer had been discussed by all the major Zionist leaders during the 1920s, 1930s, and 1940s, but they could not bring themselves to turn it into policy – and yet once the shooting started in 1948, it quickly became something very like policy.

In the words of Benny Morris, the leading Israeli historian of the "new generation" on what happened to the Palestinian refugees in 1948: "No doubt, Arab fright and flight [in 1948] were leavened by reports of real and imagined atrocities – and there were many real ones. . . . Pillage [by Jewish fighters] was almost de rigueur, rape was not infrequent, the execution of prisoners of war was fairly routine during the months before April 1948 [the country was under British administration and Haganah had no POW camps], and small- and medium-scale massacres [of Arabs] occurred during April, May, July and October to November. Altogether, there were some two dozen cases" (*The Guardian*, June 14, 2004). Morris goes on to say that while the Palestinian leadership opposed Arab flight in principle, they did encourage or order many villages "to send away their women, children and old folk, to be out of harm's way. Whole villages, especially in the Jewish-dominated coastal plain, were also ordered to evacuate." So the deed was done, even though it was never officially ordered. Some of the things that the Palestinian authorities did eased the Israelis' task, but the basic fact was that the new state of Israel had only a couple of hundred thousand Arabs living within its frontiers at the ceasefire, no longer almost a million. Whatever reason the refugees left for, if you don't let them come home again when the shooting stops, it is still ethnic cleansing. But Israel could not have been a Jewish state if the majority of the Palestinian Arabs had not fled or been driven out, and it could not have remained a Jewish state if they had been allowed to return to their homes in 1949.

"We must do everything to ensure they [the Palestinian refugees] never do return."

– David Ben-Gurion's diary, July 18, 1948

Israel still cannot let them come back without ceasing to be a Jewish state, but they are not far away. Both the Israeli and the Palestinian population have grown massively in the past sixty years, the former mostly by immigration, the latter thanks to a high birth-rate, and today there are 10 million people in the territory of the former British mandate of Palestine, between the Jordan River and the sea. Five and a half million of them are Israeli Jews, and 4.5 million are Palestinian Arabs. About 1 million of the Palestinians, the descendants of those who were not forced out in 1948, live within Israel, and the rest live under Israeli military occupation no more than a couple of hours' drive away (not counting the checkpoints and road-blocks) in the rest of former Palestine, in territories that Israel conquered in 1967. By 2010, the numbers of Jews and Arabs in Palestine will be equal, and by 2015, the Arabs will have regained the majority they lost at the end of the 1940s. The expulsion of Palestinians in 1948 cannot be reversed if Israel is to survive, but if Israel is not to end up as a classic settler state, ruling permanently over an oppressed majority of another nation, it has to relinquish the territories it took in the 1967 war.

For the first twenty years after its independence, Israel lived in a state of siege, surrounded by hostile Arab armies, but the Six-Day War of 1967 changed all that. Its borders were pushed much farther away, the military threat from the neighbouring Arab states gradually faded – and most of the Palestinian refugees of 1948 found themselves back under Israel's control. Israel didn't want them back, of course; the whole point was to have a Jewish state, not a binational one. But on the other hand, it would be nice to keep the land . . .

The arguments that began in the Israeli cabinet on the morrow of the 1967 victories have never been settled, nor have they ever stopped for long. Should Israel hand back all the conquered lands in return for a permanent peace with all its neighbours? Should it hang on to at least the West Bank and the Gaza Strip, which had been part of mandatory Palestine under the British and are seen by many Jews as part of their historic homeland? And if it does hold on to those territories, what about all the Palestinian Arabs who live there? The moment after a great victory is usually when the worst mistakes are made, and this was no exception. The first Jewish settlements in the West Bank sprang up within months, and for the next forty years opportunity after opportunity to trade these lands for peace was wasted while the Israelis argued amongst themselves about how much of the conquered territories, if any, should be returned.

That sounds a bit harsh, but I suspect that any Zionist leader from the late nineteenth century or the first half of the twentieth century – Theodor Herzl, Chaim Weizmann, David Ben-Gurion, maybe even Ze'ev Jabotinsky – would deliver an even harsher judgment. Israel was a gamble against long historical odds to create a European-style state as a national homeland for Jews in the heart of the Arab world, and guarantee it a permanent future there. The first phase of the operation had to be military, since the Arabs were not going to give their territory away voluntarily, and that phase, which lasted until the late 1960s, went amazingly well. The second phase, once Israel was militarily secure, would involve finding ways to reconcile the Arabs to Israel's presence and integrate the country into the region, for otherwise its future would always be uncertain and even military threats might eventually re-emerge. Israel has done much less well at this task.

In 1967, Israel won an extraordinary military victory, quadrupling the area the country controlled in just six days of fighting. Many people in Israel, including members of Prime Minister Levi Eshkol's own cabinet, realized at once that this victory could be the lever Israel needed to extract diplomatic recognition from the Arab countries and win acceptance as a permanent part of the Middle Eastern political scenery. All it had to do was trade the land it had conquered for the peace it craved.

There were those who doubted that it could ever be done. As David Ben-Gurion said: "If I was an Arab leader I would never make [peace] with Israel. That is natural. We have taken their country." But the optimists were not wrong in believing that Israel's crushing victory in 1967 had created the raw material from which a peace deal could be fashioned. At the time, the Palestinian refugees were hardly a political factor – the Palestine Liberation Organization (PLO) had been founded some years before, but had not yet won real independence from the Arab states on whose territory it operated – and the neighbouring Arab states wanted their territory back.

In due course, two of the neighbours did make peace with Israel: Egypt in 1978, in return for the recovery of its territory in the Sinai peninsula, and Jordan in 1994. Jordan got nothing at all in return, however, because it no longer laid claim to the territories it had lost in 1967. (Jordan's King Abdullah I had annexed the West Bank and East Jerusalem after the 1948 war, rather than allowing the Palestinian state that had been authorized by the UN partition resolution to come into existence in the parts of Palestine that had not been conquered by Israel. His son, King Hussein, then compounded the error by blundering into the 1967 war after Egypt and Syria had already been defeated and losing those territories to Israel. Finally, he relinquished Jordan's claim to sovereignty over the territories to the Palestine Liberation Organization in 1988.)

The peace treaties with Egypt and Jordan took the military pressure off Israel, but it never managed to make peace with the Palestinian Arabs who were the real victims of the country's creation in 1948, nor with Syria, whose land on the Golan Heights overlooking northern Israel has also been occupied by Israel for forty years. The latent state of war between Israel and the Arab states was prolonged for another long generation, and continues to this day. Israelis can find a hundred arguments to explain why it's the Arabs' fault that the other peace deals didn't happen, but the indisputable fact is that the Israelis themselves could never agree to a "land for peace" deal over these territories because some of them were committed to planting Jewish settlements all over them.

Now the settlements are there – around 450,000 Jews in former East Jerusalem and the West Bank, and 17,000 on the Golan Heights – and they constitute a huge impediment to a land-for-peace deal. It took decades for a majority of Israelis to come around to the "two-state solution" originally envisaged by the 1948 UN resolution, the notion that lasting peace would not be possible unless the Palestinians had their own state too. It has taken them more decades to accept that that Palestinian state would have to have all the territory beyond Israel's pre-1967 borders, including East Jerusalem. In fact, they have still not accepted it, and time is running out. Israelis used to say of the late Yasser Arafat, founder of Fatah in 1958 and leader of the

PLO from 1969 until his death in 2004, that he "never missed an opportunity to miss an opportunity," and that's quite true. But for Israel to miss a forty-year-long window of opportunity is an accomplishment that puts Arafat's in the shade.

There had to be one more war, in 1973, before the Arab states around Israel accepted the lesson of 1967 and stopped trying to match Israel militarily. Another decade passed in shaping and implementing the peace deal with Egypt (for which President Anwar Sadat was assassinated by Islamist radicals three years after the treaty was signed, in 1981), and in almost-but-never-quite-successful attempts to negotiate a similar deal with Syria. But by the early 1980s, the spotlight was already shifting to the Palestinians. Which was as it should be, because the fate of the people who had paid the price for the creation of Israel was always the core of the problem.

For more than two decades, from the mid-1960s to the late 1980s, the PLO and allied groups carried out sporadic terrorist attacks both in Israel and abroad, with the primary goal of re-branding the so-called "refugees" as "Palestinians." It was the necessary first step in re-establishing a claim over at least part of the lost lands, because "refugees," as Israeli propaganda and the Western media used to call them, were nondescript, generic Arabs who could by implication easily be resettled somewhere else in the broad reaches of the Arab world, whereas "Palestinians" were people who had a specific right to the land of Palestine. But as early as 1974 Yasser Arafat intimated, in the first ever speech to the UN General Assembly by the representative of a non-governmental organization, that his final goal was a deal with Israel that gave the Palestinians a state too: "Today I have come bearing an olive branch and a freedom fighter's gun. Do not let the olive branch fall from my hand." By the end of the 1970s, the PLO was largely out of the terrorism business (although some fringe Palestinian organizations that rejected his authority continued their attacks), but the Israelis went on trying to kill Arafat until at least 1985, when an air raid on his headquarters, then in Tunisia, killed seventy-three people. (Arafat escaped because he had gone out jogging.)

Despite a blank Israeli refusal to contemplate the possibility of a Palestinian state (it was illegal for any Israeli to have contact with the PLO until 1993), Arafat moved world public opinion steadily towards acceptance of a "two-state solution" in the course of the 1980s. He was indirectly assisted by the outbreak of the first intifada in late 1987 (the "war of the stones," as some call it), when Palestinian resentment at the endless humiliations and occasional brutalities of the Israeli military occupation boiled over in an unarmed and largely spontaneous uprising. More than a thousand Palestinians were killed in the next five years, including 241 children, and 160 Israelis also died. The political impact of the intifada was huge, persuading the rest of the world and even most Israelis that "something" had to be done about the Palestinians.

Yasser Arafat could not take credit for the intifada (although he tried), but he understood that it had created an environment in which a Palestinian state was coming to be seen as a potential solution to a problem that even Israelis could no longer deny or ignore. In December 1988, he made his historic speech accepting UN Security Council Resolution 242, promising future recognition of Israel, and renouncing "terrorism in all its forms, including state terrorism." And although he did not say it in so many words (he had his own public opinion to consider), by accepting 242 he was implicitly accepting Israel within its pre-1967 borders, and accepting also that a Palestinian state would be confined to the territories that Israel had conquered in that war. It was precisely what Israel had been waiting to hear for all those years. Or at least, it was what Israel *should* have been waiting to hear. In fact, it took another five years, because the Likud Party, which still opposed any contact with the PLO and strongly backed the settler movement, won the 1988 elections. It was only after Labour won the 1992 elections under the leadership of Yitzhak Rabin, a former general with a hawkish reputation, that contacts began between the Israeli government and the PLO. These culminated in the Oslo accords of September 1993.

"I enter negotiations with Chairman Arafat, the leader of the PLO, the representative of the Palestinian people, with the purpose to have co-existence between our two entities, Israel as a Jewish state and [a] Palestinian state, entity, next to us, living in peace."

– Prime Minister Yitzhak Rabin on
Larry King Live, CNN, June 1995

Serious negotiations on a two-state solution lasted, at intervals, from 1993 to 2000. There was huge opposition from much of the Israeli right, which wanted to hold on to the occupied territories forever, and equally from Palestinian "rejectionists" who did not want to concede Israel's right to rule almost four-fifths of former Palestine. The latter, who were mostly concentrated in the new Islamist political movements, Hamas and Islamic Jihad, launched an unprecedented wave of suicide-bomb attacks in Israel in 1994–95 in an attempt to derail the negotiations by turning the Israeli public against them, but the deal might still have been done if Rabin had not been assassinated by a Jewish opponent of the Oslo accords in 1995. Both Arafat, the former terrorist and national hero of the Palestinian cause, and Rabin, the former hawk and hero-commander of the 1967 war, had enough credibility with their respective communities to be able to push the historic compromise through.

After Rabin's murder, however, the process stalled. Initially it was assumed that Rabin's successor, Shimon Peres, would win the next election easily on a sympathy vote, but the Palestinian Islamists recognized that the right-wing Likud Party was their "objective ally" in trying to prevent a two-state solution. During the election campaign they redoubled their suicide-bomb attacks, targeting mostly crowded buses, in an attempt to stir hatred and distrust of the Palestinians and of those Israelis who wanted to deal with them and to drive Israeli voters into the arms of Likud. They succeeded: Peres very narrowly lost the May 1996 election. The new Likud government, led by Binyamin Netanyahu, paid lip-service to the Oslo accords (mainly in order to placate the United States, then led by President Bill Clinton), but dragged its feet endlessly on implementation. And the Islamist suicide attacks, unsurprisingly, died down. In the two and a half years when Arafat and Rabin or his successor, Shimon Peres, were actively negotiating for a two-state peace settlement, there were thirteen mass attacks on Israeli civilians, all but one on buses, bus stops, or bus terminals, killing 47 people in 1994, 39 people in 1995, and 59 people during the election campaign in early 1996. Once Netanyahu was safely in power and the risk of a peace settlement subsided, there were no further bus-bomb attacks, and only two attacks of any kind in the next three years in which more than three Israelis were killed.

In three years in power, Netanyahu managed to avoid ever getting to the "third stage withdrawals" of Israeli troops from large parts of the occupied territories that the Oslo Interim Agreement of 1995 had scheduled for July 1997, and there were never substantive negotiations between his government and the PLO on the future of the Jewish settlements in the territories. Indeed, Netanyahu's years in office were characterized by a surge in building activity to expand existing Jewish settlements in the Palestinian territories and found new ones, in order to create "facts on the ground" that it would be very hard for any subsequent Israeli government to undo. As Ariel Sharon, then foreign minister, told a group of right-wing militants in 1998: "Everybody has to move, run and grab as many hilltops as they can to enlarge the settlements because everything we take now will stay ours. . . . Everything we don't grab will go to them." This not only sapped Palestinian faith in the "peace process"; it was almost certainly intended to do exactly that. But in mid-1999, Netanyahu lost power to Ehud Barak, an ex-general and Labour Party activist who cobbled together an extremely diverse coalition and launched one last big push for a peace settlement based on the Oslo accords.

The summit meeting between Arafat, Barak, and President Clinton at Camp David in July 2000 was seen as a make-or-break moment by the latter two, although not by Arafat. Barak rightly judged that he could not get any peace agreement that the Palestinians would accept past his own fragile cabinet, but calculated that if he could get a single, global agreement on all the outstanding issues he could go over their heads and put the package to the Israeli public in a referendum that might well succeed. Clinton had only six months left in office and was in legacy mode: a Middle East peace settlement would go far to erase the memory of oral sex in the White House. It's not clear whether Arafat understood how much in a hurry the other two men were, however, and he was not under similar pressure himself. Despite the erosion of Palestinian support for a compromise settlement during the seven years of very slow progress, steady expansion of Israeli settlements, and Arafat's own corrupt and capricious leadership of the Palestinian Authority, he was still managing to keep most Palestinians united behind his strategy.

The Camp David summit is highly controversial, since in retrospect it is seen as the turning point after which hopes for a peace settlement rapidly evaporated on both sides. The story put out both by Barak and, indirectly, by Clinton after the failure of the summit suggested that Israel had made an unprecedentedly generous offer for a final settlement, which Arafat turned down flat, choosing instead to return to terrorism. In some versions, this story is embellished with the detail that Arafat had not realized that Israel would never allow the Palestinians who had been driven out in 1948 and their descendants to return to their homes – after more than thirty years on the case! – and that that was the deal-breaker. In any case, it was all Arafat's fault, and what it proved was that Israel "had nobody to negotiate with." This interpretation now has the force of divine writ in Israeli political mythology, and although Arafat died in 2004 it is still used by people in every part of the political spectrum to explain why Israel must act unilaterally and *impose* a peace settlement on the Palestinians.

What actually happened on July 18, 2000, was that Clinton read out his proposal for a final settlement (largely written by the Israelis), according to which a demilitarized Palestinian state would be created incorporating all of the Gaza Strip and

73 per cent of the West Bank. After a period lasting from ten to twenty-five years, most of the rest of the West Bank would also revert to Palestine, but Israel would permanently annex 9 per cent of it, including most of the major settlement blocks and a corridor of land connecting the Jewish settlements east of Jerusalem with the settlements and military installations in the Jordan valley facing the kingdom of Jordan. A demilitarized Palestinian state would get a bridge or tunnel across or under this corridor to connect the northern and southern halves of the West Bank, and receive partial compensation for the lands lost to Jewish settlements in the West Bank in the form of about one-ninth as much territory from Israel proper – a specific parcel of land that turned out to be a strip of desert adjacent to the Gaza Strip used as a dump for toxic waste. On the thorny question of Jerusalem, the Palestinians would be allowed to have their capital in a distant suburb of the city, and would be given sovereignty over the Muslim and Christian quarters of the Old City, but they would only have "custodianship" over Temple Mount. Palestinian refugees living elsewhere would have the right to move to the new Palestinian state, but no "right of return" to Israel proper.

After Clinton had finished, Arafat said no. The U.S. president banged the table and said, "You are leading your people and the region to a catastrophe." A formal Palestinian rejection of the U.S.–Israeli proposals the next day marked the effective end of the summit, and the game of laying the blame for its failure began. The Israelis won it hands down in the Western media, with much help from a disappointed Bill Clinton, but that doesn't mean their version was correct.

The basic Palestinian position was that they had made their concessions when they signed the interim Oslo accords in 1993, accepting the permanent loss of the 78 per cent of mandatory Palestine that had been seized by Israel in 1948 in return for the right to build an independent state on the remaining 22 per cent. When they were confronted at Camp David with a further Israeli demand to keep 27 per cent of the West Bank in the short run and almost a tenth of it in the long run, they rejected it out of hand. (Israeli sources often claim that they offered the Palestinians 96 per cent of the West Bank within a quarter-century, but they achieve this figure by omitting the land around east Jerusalem that Israel had annexed.) The Palestinian negotiators can be criticized for failing to make detailed counter-proposals at Camp David, but they did accept in principle the notion that Israel might annex some West Bank territory in order to keep some of its settlements – provided that Palestine was compensated with Israeli land "of equal size and value," and that the land ceded to Israel should not affect the contiguity of their own land or lead to the incorporation of Palestinians into Israel. As for the question of the "right of return," allegedly the deal-breaker, it was barely discussed at all. The Palestinians had warned before the summit that it was unrealistic to expect to achieve a final settlement in a single meeting and that it should be regarded as the first of a series, and their behaviour, while maladroit, did not amount to a rejection of further negotiations.

Further negotiations were largely pre-empted, however, by Likud Party leader Ariel Sharon's provocative visit to Haram al-Sharif/Temple Mount in Jerusalem, accompanied by about a thousand Israeli policemen, on September 28, 2000. Both Palestinian and American officials, informed in advance of Sharon's intentions, had urged Barak to ban the visit, for in Palestinian eyes Sharon was the epitome of the hard-line

Israeli Arab-killer. From his command of Unit 101 during the reprisal raids that killed several hundred Palestinian villagers in the Gaza Strip and the West Bank in the early 1950s, down to his "personal responsibility" (as assessed by the Kahan Commission, which recommended his dismissal as defence minister) for allowing the massacre of several thousand Palestinians in the Sabra and Chatila refugee camps by Maronite militiamen allied to Israel in Beirut in 1982, Sharon was connected to some of the most disturbing episodes in Palestinian–Israeli relations. But for unknown reasons, Barak refused to ban Sharon's visit to the square, during which the latter asserted that the entire complex, including the al-Aqsa mosque, the third-holiest site in Islam, would remain in Israel in perpetuity. The Palestinians in the square began to throw stones and the Israeli police replied with tear gas and rubber bullets, but nobody was killed until a much larger demonstration after Friday prayers on the following day, when Israeli security forces killed four Palestinians and wounded more than two hundred, and the second intifada was born.

Ehud Barak has always maintained that Sharon's visit to the square was an attempt to discredit him and his "soft" approach to the Palestinians, and that is certainly true. Others insist that Sharon was deliberately trying to provoke Palestinian violence by his extremely intrusive, high-profile visit to a location sacred to Muslims, with the aim of aborting any further Israeli–Palestinian negotiations, and that may well be true too. The official Israeli line is that Yasser Arafat had been lying all along, and deliberately returned to violence after turning down an incredibly generous Israeli peace offer at Camp David, taking advantage of Sharon's little faux-pas. This makes no sense at all. Sharon was one of the wiliest and least naive politicians in

Israel, and did not visit the square in a moment of absent-mindedness; he was certainly aware that any upsurge in Palestinian violence would work in his favour politically, as he was seen as a tough leader who "knew how to deal with the Arabs." Arafat had dedicated the previous dozen years to the pursuit of a Palestinian state as part of a two-state solution, at considerable risk to his own life, and had no reason to believe that negotiations with Barak's government were at an end. But they were, and it was Sharon's visit to the square that effectively ended them.

The Camp David negotiations might have worked, but they didn't. There was a final round of talks on a negotiated Israeli–Palestinian peace settlement in Washington, Cairo, and finally Taba, Egypt, in December 2000 and January 2001, a time when Clinton and Barak both had only weeks left in office. The participants came a lot closer to agreement than they had at Camp David the previous July, by all accounts, but it was still a largely symbolic event as neither the American nor the Israeli leader could bind his successor. And that, in retrospect, was the end of the search for the two-state solution, at least for this generation.

The second (al-Aqsa) intifada differed from the first in that many more weapons were used by the Palestinians, and as a result the kill ratio was not so lopsided: only four Palestinians died for every Israeli, as opposed to the ten-to-one ratio of the first intifada. By the time it subsided in 2005, more than 4,000 Palestinians and 1,000 Israelis had been killed. It served as a dramatic demonstration that the era of the Oslo accords had come to an end, but it was much more effect than cause. What really defined the new era, from the Israeli perspective, was the landslide victory of Ariel Sharon in an election in February

2001 that was precipitated by the collapse of Barak's cabinet. Sharon pledged to achieve "security and true peace" while insisting he would not be bound by previous negotiations with the Palestinians and would not meet with Yasser Arafat.

In practice, Sharon was completely uninterested in negotiations with the Palestinians within the framework of the Oslo accords, preferring unilateral actions like the Wall ("security fence") that he began building in the West Bank along approximately the line of the new border that Israel had proposed in the Camp David talks, which incorporated all the larger Jewish settlements into Israel. Its justification was that it stopped terrorist attacks, and it was undoubtedly effective in that respect, but its course suggested strongly that it was intended to solidify over time into a new frontier for Israel. And meanwhile, in the occupied territories, traditional support for the PLO was rapidly eroding in favour of Hamas and the other "rejectionist" Islamist organizations, as Palestinians lost faith both in the possibility of a negotiated peace and in the ability of the deeply corrupt Palestinian Authority to reform itself. But people on both sides were and still are reluctant to acknowledge the implication of their choices, which is that there will be another generation of Israeli military domination of and constant incursions into the Palestinian occupied territories, which are turning into large, open-air prisons (especially Gaza, which has all its borders sealed by the Israelis) – and, quite possibly, a new generation of international war as well.

It was at this point, with the "peace process" completely dead, that the Israeli politicians of Likud who had done the most to kill it finally began to worry about the demographic implications of keeping all the area from the sea to the Jordan River under perpetual Israeli control. If you did not permit the emergence of an independent and democratic Palestinian state in which the Palestinian population of the West Bank, the Gaza Strip, and east Jerusalem enjoyed full political and human rights, then they would be bound to seek those rights in the broader context of old mandatory Palestine, an area that has in practice been back under one supreme authority, that of the Israeli government and army, ever since 1967. And there will soon be more Arabs than Jews in that area.

"We are approaching the point where more and more Palestinians will say: 'We have been won over. We agree with [National Union Leader Avigdor] Lieberman. There is no room for two states between Jordan and the sea. All that we want is the right to vote.' The day they do that is the day we lose everything."

– Deputy Prime Minister Ehud Olmert, (Prime minister 2006–present), *Yedioth Ahronoth* newspaper, November 2003

This belated recognition of the long-term demographic threat to a purely Jewish state did not produce a last-minute conversion to the two-state project among the Likud leaders who had been fighting against it for most of their lives. Instead, they opted for no state for the Palestinians, but a rigorous separation of the two populations (except for Israel's own Arab population, which they had no legal right to segregate), and perpetual Israeli military supervision over the Palestinian enclaves in the West Bank and the Gaza Strip. (This was formally known as "disengagement.") In the West Bank and east Jerusalem, this separation could be accomplished mostly by the Wall, with the withdrawal of some outlying Jewish settlements that could not practically be included within it; in the tiny, highly congested Gaza Strip, it required the closure of all the Jewish settlements (some eight thousand people). Even this was too much for many Likud activists, who insist that all of "Eretz Israel" is sacred Jewish territory, but Sharon forced them to accept his unilateral dismantling of the Jewish settlements in the Gaza Strip and four tiny ones in the northern West Bank in the summer of 2005. Soon after, he broke with Likud entirely and founded a new party, Kadima ("Forward"), which united the less ideological parts of the right with the despairing centre and centre-left. Sharon was disabled by a stroke in early 2006, but in the March 2006 election, Kadima, now under the leadership of Ehud Olmert, emerged as the largest party and formed a coalition government that continues to pursue the "disengagement" strategy.

In this context, it was hardly surprising when the most prominent "rejectionists" on the Palestinian side, the Hamas organization, also emerged as the victors in the parliamentary elections of January 2006. The elections demonstrated beyond a reasonable doubt that the Palestinians were giving up on the two-state solution, too. Hamas quite explicitly urges Palestinians not to make defeatist and unnecessary compromises with the "Zionist entity" now, but to wait until the balance of forces, demographic or military, allows them to reclaim their entire heritage, the land of Palestine. At that point, they say, within a state reaching from the Jordan to the sea that is both democratic and Islamic, there would be room and full religious and civil rights for Jews who wished to remain – but realistically, Hamas does not expect most Jews to stay in a state where they would no longer be the majority and control all the levers of power.

The elections were free and fair, but the Palestinians had made the wrong choice: the Israeli government, Canada, the

United States, and the European Union refused to have anything to do with a "terrorist" organization, even if it had won the democratic right to form a Palestinian government. Israel even withheld the customs revenues due to the Palestinian Authority, its main source of income, which caused great hardship in the occupied territories, where living standards had already been in free-fall for some years as a result of continual border closures and the loss of Palestinian jobs within Israel proper. The subsequent mini–civil war among the Palestinians in June 2007, which left Hamas in control of the Gaza Strip and Fatah still in charge of the West Bank, eliminated any remaining possibility of a negotiated, comprehensive "two-state" peace settlement for the foreseeable future. It is finally true that Israel has "nobody to negotiate with"—at least nobody who can deliver the goods.

They missed the bus, the page has turned, whatever simile you prefer, but that era is over, and it isn't coming back for a long time, if ever. Israelis and Palestinians, and by extension most other people in the Middle East as well, plus the United States if it chooses to stay involved, are back in the world of irreconcilable ambitions, of non-negotiable demands, and perhaps of regional war. The Palestinians have chosen this route out of despair (if "chosen" is really the right word). The Israelis have chosen it on the basis of a fundamental miscalculation of Israel's ability to dominate the entire region strategically in the long term.

The Palestinian leadership may withdraw its offer, having concluded . . . that . . . it will never be enough for an adversary that seems to want all.

The Hamas rejectionists, and/or those, secular as well as religious, who think like them, may take over the leadership. The whole, broader, Arab-Israeli peace process which Anwar Sadat began, and which came to be seen as irreversible, may prove to be reversible after all. In which case, the time may also come when the cost to the U.S. of continuing to support its infinitely importunate protégé in a never-ending conflict against an ever-widening circle of adversaries is greater than its will and resources to sustain it.

— David Hirst, *The Observer*, September 21, 2003

We are already at least halfway to the destination David Hirst sketched out in 2003. Israel has dominated the entire Middle East strategically ever since 1967, and its close alliance with the United States plus the sheer weakness of the Arab states helped to extend that domination into the early twenty-first century. But Israel's ability to ignore the wishes of the Palestinians and those of all its Arab neighbours rests on three strategic assets, none of which is likely to last forever. One is its monopoly of nuclear weapons within the region, now around forty years old. Israel has at least several hundred nuclear weapons, and a variety of delivery vehicles able to reach every Arab country (plus Iran, of course), whereas no other state in the Middle East has any. The second is the overwhelming military superiority of its conventional armed forces, which could still easily destroy the regular armies of all the neighbouring Arab states. The third is the unstinting, almost unconditional military and financial support of the world's sole superpower, the United States. A fourth asset, not of Israel's making, is the sheer poverty, incompetence, and disunity of the Arab states in its immediate vicinity.

Israel's problem is that none of these strategic assets is permanent. Technically, its regional monopoly of nuclear weapons has already been broken by Pakistan, a nuclear-armed Muslim country whose weapons have the range to threaten Israel if it ever chose to do so, but Pakistan under the current management is not seen by Israel as part of the local strategic equation. Iran, on the other hand, is very definitely part of the local equation, which is why the Israelis have put so much political effort into persuading the United States to take the threat of Iranian nuclear weapons seriously.

When the Israeli government took its original decision to develop nuclear weapons (with clandestine French and British aid) in the late 1950s, they were primarily seen as a last-ditch weapon to be used only if the country were being overrun by victorious Arab armies. In technical terms, the strategy that the weapons then served is known as finite or limited deterrence: the sole purpose of Israel's nuclear weapons was to prevent the military destruction of the Israeli state. By the time the Israeli deterrent force was fully in operation in the early 1970s, however, that threat was fading fast.

By their dismal performances in the 1967 and 1973 wars, the Arab armies surrounding Israel had conclusively proved to their own governments that they could not beat the Israelis. As a result, those governments gradually ceased even to buy the kind of weapons that would enable their armed forces to fight Israel on a basis of technological equality, so Israel's "finite deterrent" was no longer really needed. But the weapons were not dismantled, of course; they just morphed into the foundation for a strategy of extended deterrence. These nuclear weapons, along with "undeclared offensive chemical warfare capabilities" and "an undeclared offensive biological warfare program" (according to a report released in June 2000 by the Office of Technology Assessment of the U.S. Congress), are believed by the Israelis to deter the country's Arab and Iranian neighbours from doing all sorts of other undesirable things well short of trying to "drive the Jews into the sea." As Shimon Peres, currently deputy prime minister and one of the country's most senior political figures, once put it, "acquiring a superior weapons system would mean the possibility of using it for compellent purposes – that is, forcing the other side to accept Israeli political demands."

It is a desire not to lose this capacity for extended deterrence, rather than a fear that Israel's cities will start disappearing under mushroom clouds the moment some neighbour acquires nuclear weapons, that drives current Israeli policy towards Iran. Even if Iran acquired a few nuclear bombs one of these days, Israel's capacity to retaliate against an Iranian attack by virtually exterminating Iran would be quite undamaged. Its nuclear striking forces are well dispersed among a number of different delivery vehicles and are not vulnerable to a surprise attack, so simple, finite deterrence against Iran would still work (provided that the Iranian regime is not under the control of suicidal maniacs, which it does not appear to be). But Israel's huge, largely invisible ability to threaten all its neighbours with the apocalypse if they get out of line would be gone in an instant. Israel, too, would be deterred.

It is the prospective loss of "deterrence" in that extended sense that really concerns Israel's senior military and political leaders, not some feverish nightmare about an Iranian nuclear attack. No matter what scare stories they may serve up to frighten the public, Israeli generals understand the strategic realities. But whatever they do, extended deterrence is a weapon that is bound to fall from Israel's hand eventually. Even if Iran is not really seeking nuclear weapons at this time, or if a massive American air assault eliminates Iran's nuclear potential for a number of years, some other state in the region is likely to get nuclear weapons sooner or later, and just one would break Israel's nuclear monopoly. That's one strategic asset gone.

The second asset, Israel's absolute superiority over any or all of its neighbours in conventional (i.e., non-nuclear) warfare, is already eroding rapidly. It's not that the Arab states are buying large quantities of advanced conventional weapons again – they are not – but that the prevailing mode of war in the region has shifted, much to the disadvantage of Israel's classic "blitzkrieg" style of warfare. The tanks-mechanized infantry-air power combination, designed to slice through enemy formations as much by speed as by firepower and technological superiority, was perfectly suited to Israel's dependence on a rapidly mobilized citizen army of reservists. It could deliver enormous numbers of soldiers to the front in a matter of hours (Israel has actually enjoyed numerical superiority over the Arab armies it faced at the front in every war it has fought except the first one, in 1948), but it could not afford to keep its citizen soldiers there for months or years, as the economy would collapse. So long as the primary mode of war was high-tech conventional armies fighting each other across borders and other front lines, Israel won the wars easily – but the last time it fought an Arab army in that fashion was more than thirty years ago.

Now the Israeli army's primary tasks are those of an occupation army and a counter-guerrilla force, which are things that citizen armies do distinctly less well. Even professional soldiers like guerrilla wars less and fight them worse than conventional wars, because the danger is low-grade but invisible and constant, and there is never anything that emotionally resembles victory. Counter-insurgency operations ultimately corrupt almost all armies and sap their professionalism:

discipline slackens, abuses grow, and distinctions between innocent civilians and guerrilla fighters blur and fade. To the average Israeli conscript serving his time in the occupied territories, there is no such thing as an innocent Palestinian, just as to the average U.S. Marine Corps private in Anbar province in Iraq there is no such thing as an innocent Iraqi. You really can't blame them, because they cannot tell the difference between those who plan to kill them and those who merely hate them, and besides they are barely out of childhood themselves and they are very frightened. But the result is a steep decline in the army's fitness to do other, harder things.

"This will be a disaster for Israel. [Sheikh Hassan Nasrallah, leader of Hezbollah] will be seen in the world as someone who fired thousands of Katyushas at Israeli communities for weeks and came out unscathed."
– Moshe Arens, former Israeli defence and foreign minister, in
Ha'aretz, July 2006

The consequences for the Israeli army of thirty years of occupation duty were shockingly on display during the 2006 war in southern Lebanon. The whole purpose of the war, from the point of view of the Israeli general staff, was to re-establish Israel's conventional military deterrence, the long-established principle that Israel might and probably would reply to any attack with a disproportionate response. There was a sense both in the Likud government and the armed forces that this deterrent principle of "a dozen eyes for an eye" had been seriously undermined by a number of years of failure to impose that proportion of casualties on either the Palestinians or on Hezbollah in southern Lebanon, so a pretext was being sought to deliver a lesson. When the pretext duly presented itself,

however, the Israeli army proved incapable of administering
the lesson. One reason for the lower casualty rate, it turned out,
was that Hezbollah had copies of Israeli aerial photo-
reconnaissance pictures with the bunkers they had identified
clearly marked in Hebrew – so Hezbollah moved its fighters to
other bunkers as soon as the war began. (It is assumed in
southern Lebanon that Israeli border guards traded the photos
for commercial quantities of drugs.) Hezbollah's fighters were
not driven from their positions despite weeks of bombing,
and the Israeli infantry, when they were finally committed to
the battle, were unable to dislodge them either. The end result
was to leave Israel's army looking less effective than Arabs had
believed, not more, and to inspire many Arabs with the novel
thought – novel since the 1970s, at least – that maybe Israel
could be beaten militarily.

That is not true. *No* country with a large stock of nuclear
weapons can be beaten militarily. If it starts to lose a conventional war in a terminal way, out come its nuclear weapons and
everybody dies. It is extremely dangerous for Arabs to believe
that Israel can be beaten militarily – but it would be entirely
logical for the Arabs to seek nuclear weapons, so that they, too,
could not be beaten militarily. And in the meantime, the hope
spreads in the Muslim Middle East that the Israeli army could
be worn down by low-tech guerrilla movements within the
occupied territories and along its borders. For the first time
since the 1970s, some Arabs who aren't delusional religious
fanatics seriously think that Israel could eventually be defeated
militarily in this way. The second of Israel's indispensable
strategic assets, its unquestionable superiority in conventional
warfare, has become a doubtful and endangered commodity.

Israel's third and most important asset, the unquestioning

support of the U.S. public and government, is now also at risk. Since the end of the Cold War, it has depended not on a true convergence of U.S. and Israeli strategic interests but on a brilliantly successful political operation to convince Americans that the old verities still hold true. In fact, there is almost no American strategic or political objective in the Middle East in all that time, from the first President Bush's administration to George W.'s time in office, that critically depended on Israeli military or political support, and there are a great many that would have been easier to achieve if the United States had not been so closely tied to Israel. Countries choose their allies for a variety of reasons, some of them more emotional than coldly rational, and it is conceivable that the American public would support the Israeli alliance even if they understood that it was a strategic liability – but nobody in a position of power in Israel trusts American goodwill enough to want to find out if that is true or not. Many Americans are sentimental about Israel; very few Israelis, except those of American origin, are sentimental about the United States.

The American Israel Public Affairs Committee (AIPAC) and other pro-Israeli lobbies are legendary for their ability to manipulate the U.S. Congress, and it is a measure of Israel's invulnerability to the usual criteria for good behaviour on the part of U.S. allies that numbers of Americans have been jailed for long periods for spying on the United States on Israel's behalf without this having any discernible impact on the U.S.–Israel strategic relationship. Indeed, the U.S.–Israel relationship under President George W. Bush has been so close that in 2005 Bush broke with thirty-eight years of American policy by abandoning U.S. support for United Nations Resolutions 242 and 338, the basic international documents on the subject of the Palestinian occupied territories. Praising Ariel Sharon as a "man of peace," he declared that at least some of the Jewish settlements would have to remain within Israel in any Palestinian–Israeli peace agreement. But the United States remains a sovereign state, and realists in Israel have always been aware that the American alliance is not graven in stone. The time when that alliance begins to be questioned in the United States may be about to arrive.

Several factors are coming together to jeopardize Israel's privileged relationship with the United States. One is a growing desire on the part of the American public to have as little as possible to do with the perennial and intractable problems of the Middle East. It is driven mainly by the fact that U.S. soldiers are now dying in significant numbers in the region in a war that, more than half of Americans now believe, has nothing to do with the "war on terror." And this growing opinion will not just vanish when U.S. troops finally leave Iraq. The public's memory is short, but it is not that short.

In early 2004, Yossi Sarid, a senior member of the Knesset's defence and foreign affairs committee, told the Associated Press: "It was known in Israel that the story that [Iraq had] weapons of mass destruction [that] could be activated in 45 minutes was an old wives' tale. Israel didn't want to spoil President Bush's scenario, and it should have." But he said that after the Iraq adventure was already going sour. Before the invasion, Israel pushed the United States as hard as it could to invade Iraq. Israel has seriously overplayed its hand in terms of exploiting its U.S. relationship in recent years, taking advantage of the Bush administration's chronic inability to distinguish between American and Israeli interests, and it may eventually pay a high price if the American public comes to believe that U.S. troops are dying to serve Israel's purposes.

None of Israel's three strategic assets is yet in mortal danger. It may be another thirty years before any Muslim country closer than Pakistan develops nuclear weapons; the Israeli Defence Forces may heed the lessons of their recent poor performances and learn to cope with their new challenges; the United States may remain a loyal ally of Israel until the end of time. But Israelis are currently betting the future of their country on the assumption that all three of those factors will remain unchanged down to 2050. They are also betting that all of the nearby Arab countries, whose total population outnumbers Israel's by twenty-to-one, will remain so corruptly and incompetently led, so bereft of modern industry, science, and technology, and so militarily weak that they can never turn that huge numerical advantage into a strategic asset – not just for the next ten years, but for the next fifty, or indeed forever. They are basing their policy on the assumption that the strategic good times will last indefinitely. This would be regarded as poor management practice by the operator of a successful hamburger stand.

For more than thirty years, Israel's basic dilemma has been to decide whether it needs to make painful concessions to the Arabs and abandon cherished ambitions in order to get a durable peace settlement and start integrating itself into the region; or whether it can forever get away with depending on its own military strength and its powerful U.S. ally and just ignore the wishes of the Arabs. Now, the question has subtly altered: it is whether the Arab states of the ancien regime could actually deliver on commitments to peaceful relations with Israel even if their governments did make a deal. The risk of their being overthrown or otherwise replaced by Islamist regimes that have no intention of honouring a peace agreement with Israel could be just too great. In 2005, after the Muslim Brotherhood's candidates won a fifth of the seats in the Egyptian parliamentary election despite severe obstructionism by the regime, its leader, Mohamed al-Nahdy Akef, said that his movement did not recognize Israel and proposed that the peace treaty that Egypt had signed with Israel at Camp David in 1978 be put to a popular referendum. In January 2006, the Palestinians of the occupied territories gave 74 of 132 seats in parliament to the candidates of Hamas, an Islamist movement that refuses to recognize Israel or to abide by the various agreements that were signed over the past fifteen years by Israel and the Palestine Liberation Organization. The prognosis is for more of the same.

Nothing in politics is inevitable, and there's almost always another last chance farther down the road. But the Israeli–Palestinian dispute, which came tantalizingly close to a peaceful resolution in the 1990s, is now backsliding rapidly towards the 1970s, and as it intensifies it threatens to draw the rest of the region in once again. Down that road, sooner or later, lies Armageddon. The politics are so intractable, and the prospects are so appalling, that you understand why Benny Morris was tempted by the thought below, even though both his alternative apocalypses are repugnant.

"One wonders what Ben-Gurion – who probably could have engineered a comprehensive rather than a partial transfer in 1948, but refrained – would have made of all this, were he somehow resurrected. Perhaps he would now regret his restraint. Perhaps, had he gone the whole hog, today's Middle East would be a healthier, less violent place with a Jewish state between Jordan and the Mediterranean and a

Palestinian Arab state in Transjordan. Alternatively, Arab success in the 1948 war, with the Jews driven into the sea, would have obtained the same, historically calming result. Perhaps it was the very indecisiveness of the geographical and demographic outcome of 1948 that underlies the persisting tragedy of Palestine."

– Benny Morris, *The Guardian*, October 3, 2002

CHAPTER IX

CRAWLING FROM THE WRECKAGE

"*Afghanistan either has to be fixed and be peaceful, or the whole region will run into hell with us. It's not going to be like the past, that only we suffer. Those who cause us to suffer will burn in hell with us. And I hope NATO recognizes this.*"

– Afghan president Hamid Karzai,
International Herald Tribune, December 12, 2006

There is a tendency in books of this sort to predict dramatic changes on every front, and mostly changes for the worse. Hamid Karzai is playing the same game when he predicts that the whole region will "burn in hell" if he doesn't get more NATO troops and more foreign aid to turn back the revived Taliban insurgency: if you predict disaster, they may pay attention to you. But most change is not dramatic, especially in places like Afghanistan. In fact, the whole Western intervention in Afghanistan is unlikely to figure very prominently in any history of Afghanistan written later this century.

U.S. president Jimmy Carter's decision in 1979 to authorize $500 million to set up an insurgency among the conservative Afghan tribes against the pro-Soviet regime in Kabul had a huge impact on the country. Carter's national security adviser, Zbigniew Brzezinski, had persuaded him that the United States could lure the Soviet Union into a military intervention that would result in "Russia's Vietnam," and he turned out to be right. The insurgency funded and armed by the United States suckered the Soviet Union into putting troops into Afghanistan to protect the Marxist regime there, and started a chronic civil war that continues almost three decades later. But the direct Western military intervention of 2001, by contrast, has changed practically nothing.

There was never a real U.S. invasion of Afghanistan. What Washington did in 2001, sensibly enough, was to intervene in a finely balanced civil war between the Taliban regime in Kabul (almost entirely drawn from the Pashtuns, who account for about 40 per cent of the total population and are the traditionally dominant group) and a coalition of tribal forces from the various smaller ethnic groups known as the Northern Alliance. It gave the Northern Alliance lots of money and guns and it bombed the Taliban troops whenever they resisted the northerners' advance, but it let them do the fighting on the ground. This quite traditional imperial strategy worked very well – but it did mean that the United States was actually dependent on the various northern warlords for the maintenance of order after the shooting stopped. And nothing that has happened since has changed matters much, except that there are now some (non-Taliban) Pashtun warlords on the payroll, too.

The propaganda talked about bringing democracy to Afghanistan, and various democratic rituals were duly performed. A *loya jirga* was called to agree on a new constitution (but 80 per cent of the delegates were warlords). Hamid Karzai, America's choice as leader, was elected as president (but his control barely extends beyond Kabul, and some of the same warlords are in his cabinet). As for the American aid that was going to flood in and transform the country, most of it was diverted to Iraq, to be wasted there instead. So now the Taliban guerrillas are back in a big way, striking at government officials, policemen, and soldiers all over the south and southeast (the Pashtun heartland) and taking on NATO troops in open combat.

It would certainly have helped if the United States had paid attention to the job of rebuilding Afghanistan rather than diverting most available resources, military and financial, to the invasion of Iraq, but it is questionable whether it would have made enough difference to change the outcome. Foreign powers that invade Afghanistan usually fail and retreat in the end, because there really is nothing in the way of a modern state to work with there. Afghanistan is not a "failed state," it is a country in which most of the institutions we normally associate with states have not taken root in the first place. The complex networks of personal and tribal relationships that normally provide structure for the society are impenetrable to foreigners, whom most Afghans rightly mistrust after their long history of incompetent and ultimately unsuccessful foreign occupations. The current intervention was probably always destined to end in failure.

That does not necessarily mean that the eventual withdrawal of Western troops will be a disaster for Afghans. The normal ethnic balance of power in the country was gravely disrupted by the events of 2001, which left the Pashtuns largely excluded from government. (Karzai himself is Pashtun, from a clan that never had much to do with the Taliban, but his selection as president was little more than tokenism.) Integrating the Pashtuns into the government, with a fair enough share of the power and the spoils that they do not continue to support the current insurgency, means talking to the Taliban, who are far from being a monolithic bloc. This is difficult to do while the United States has an effective veto on everything Karzai does, but he has already said publicly on several occasions that he is willing to talk to Taliban groups, and he *must* eventually do this if he hopes to survive the departure of U.S. and NATO troops.

At this point in the argument, Washington tends to panic, imagining that Afghanistan will become once again the "nest of terrorists" that it thought it had stamped out in 2001. But the Taliban, distasteful though their values are to most Americans, were never the terrorists. They were the government that, out of loyalty and gratitude to Arabs like Osama bin Laden, who had fought alongside the Afghans in the long war against the Russians, gave them house-room when they had nowhere else to go. The Taliban were of course aware of al-Qaeda's Islamist convictions, which they largely shared, and probably even of its determination to attack American targets, but it is very doubtful that they were informed in advance by bin Laden of his plans for 9/11. (After all, you don't tell your hosts that you are going to do something that will get them invaded.) They have had a very unpleasant lesson in the folly of letting foreign Islamists use Afghan territory for their own purposes, and it is at least possible that they have learned something from it.

In any case, the Taliban are unlikely to come back as an exclusive Islamist, Pashtun government in the style of 1996–2001. Rather they are going to have to negotiate their place in a more traditional Afghan government that represents a balance of forces between the various ethnic groups. If Karzai is adroit enough, he can still be the leader of that government; if not, there is no shortage of candidates for the succession. The post-occupation Afghanistan will not be the fantasy of a prosperous, female-friendly, democratic society that some neo-conservatives entertained at the height of their hubris, but it will probably cause little trouble to the rest of the world.

In the Arab world, of course, there are likely to be some major changes as a result of the American defeat in Iraq, although it is not possible to predict which regimes will survive and which will go under. It's never a good idea to wish for radical change without knowing exactly what shape it will take, no matter how intolerable the present may seem, because it can *always* get worse. But change can also be for the better, and it is coming to the Middle East whether people wish it or not. The place may be hard to recognize in ten years' time, even those countries where the regime has not formally changed.

The great unsung victim of the invasion of Iraq is the United Nations, or more precisely the international law banning aggressive war that was the main reason for the creation of the UN. Caught up in the polemics about a minor colonial war in Iraq that has killed fewer American soldiers in four years than died in an average month during the Second World War, people have forgotten that the great international enterprise of the past sixty years was to create a system that frees us from the cycle of great-power wars that has blighted all of modern history. Perhaps it was too ambitious an undertaking, although the alternative is probably to accept that one day we will stumble into another world war, and this time a nuclear one. But it was well worth trying, and now the project is gravely wounded.

The core rule of the United Nations was simple: attempts to solve international disputes by force are henceforward against international law, and any gains acquired by force are illegal. Formulated in 1945, at the end of the worst war in history, the new rule was bound to be flouted by the great powers from time to time, but it provided some legal protection to small countries – and it gave the great powers an excuse to back away from confrontations among themselves, which could all too easily end in wars that would kill tens of millions. For sixty years no great power has fought any other, and even small countries have suffered fewer attacks than they used to. It may be a flimsy rule, more hope than command, but it was a step in the right direction, and because of it a great many people are alive who would otherwise be dead.

The law banning wars of aggression can sometimes be enforced by the Security Council against smaller countries, but from the start it was understood that the great powers would have to obey it voluntarily, for who could enforce it against them? Their incentive for obeying it was the knowledge that in an era of nuclear weapons they were as vulnerable to destruction in war as even the smallest country, but it was to be expected that from time to time they would break the law, and on one occasion or another almost every one of them did. No surprise there: the United Nations and the international rule of law is a hundred-year project, and in the early decades it was to be expected that the great powers would continue to resort to force illegally from time to time. But at least they generally had the decency to pretend that what they were doing was somehow covered by the law.

What has been happening in the past five years is much worse. The United States, the greatest power in the system, not only broke the law in 2003 by unilaterally invading another country, deliberately bypassing the Security Council when it was unable to get its approval for the war. In its domestic policy statements, the U.S. government now quite explicitly sets itself above international law, declaring that it will attack any country it considers a threat. This may not be a death blow to the project that the United States itself launched in 1945, but it has certainly done huge damage to it: in the Middle East, in particular, the United Nations is now regarded with little more than contempt. Even if a new American administration ends the flagrant unilateralism of the Bush years and acknowledges the role of international law, it will take a long time for the UN system to recover from the beating it has taken.

The biggest impact of the fiasco in Iraq, however, may be on the United States itself. The long-term challenges to America's position as the world's sole superpower are all in Asia, but great powers can also lose the ability to influence events and create coalitions to do large things simply because they have become discredited and mistrusted. The United States now runs a serious risk of suffering that fate – and its ability to project power in other parts of the world is being further undermined by a growing disillusionment at home with the very idea of "benevolent" foreign interventions.

"When Arabs kill Arabs and Shias kill Shias and Sunnis kill all in a spasm of violence that is blind and furious and has roots in hatreds born long before America was even a republic, to place the blame on the one player, the one country, the one military that has done more than any other to try to separate the combatants and bring conciliation is simply perverse. It infantilizes Arabs. It demonizes Americans. It wilfully overlooks the plainest of facts: Iraq is their country. We midwifed their freedom. They chose civil war."

– Charles Krauthammer, *The Washington Post*, February 2, 2007

A right-wing columnist trying to shift the responsibility for a lost war has a choice between seeking traitors at home and blaming ignorant, vicious foreigners who do not deserve the United States' help, and on the whole it is probably better for his own country's political health if people like Charles Krauthammer blame the foreigners. What is more interesting is that the American left seems ready to blame the foreigners, too.

The *Doonesbury* comic strip is an American icon, a bastion of liberal irony that runs daily in fourteen hundred newspapers around the world, and often serves as a vehicle for political or social commentary from a liberal perspective. Its writer, Gary Trudeau, never supported the invasion of Iraq, but in February 2007 he drew a series of strips that made Krauthammer look like a liberal internationalist.

In one strip an American colonel, planning the day's operation in the streets of Baghdad, notices that his Iraq army opposite number has not shown up yet, and sends a soldier to find him. Cut to the Iraqi army officer: still behind his desk, coffee cup in hand, ashtray full of cigarettes. He says to the young American soldier: "It's not in my book. Are you sure it's today?" The U.S. soldier wearily replies, "Yes, sir. You'll recall we fight every day."

Unravelling the message doesn't take a Marshall McLuhan: U.S. troops are carrying the burden of the war while lazy, cowardly Iraqis shun their duty. They don't deserve us.

Another strip was even more blatant in blaming the failure on the Iraqis. An American soldier gets behind the wheel of a Humvee and says, "Ready to do this, partner?" to the same Iraqi officer, sitting beside him in the front seat. But the Iraqi officer is asleep.

As they approach the target house, the Iraqi officer, now awake, says, "I know this house. The owner is Sunni scum."

"Well, intel wants us to capture the guy alive," says the American.

"That will not be possible. I am sworn to revenge," replies the Iraqi officer.

"Why?" asks the American. "What'd he ever do to you?"

"A member of his family killed a member of mine," replies the Iraqi, cigarette dangling from his lips.

"What? When did this happen?" asks the shocked American.

"1387," replies the Iraqi.

"What is the *matter* with you people?" screams the American.

The message is plain. These Ay-rabs are not only lazy, they are so savage that they harbour murderous grudges over six centuries. Even Americans cannot bring these people to their senses. Let's get the hell out of here. It isn't our fault that it all went wrong.

Getting out of Iraq is the least bad thing the United States can do now, and the sooner the better. If Americans must manufacture racist fantasies about the victims in order to salve their pride on the way out, then so be it, although it is a shameful, childish lie. But if you combine this growing contempt and anger in the United States towards not just Iraqis, but Arabs in general, with the strong likelihood of a popular backlash against the Israelis as the extent of their manipulation of American policy in the months leading up to the Iraq war becomes known, and factor in a general revulsion against foreign military adventures, there is a serious possibility that the United States will not only pull out of Iraq, but very substantially reduce its military presence in the entire Middle Eastern region. That would alarm the governments who have depended on its presence for so long, but it would not necessarily be a Bad Thing for the region or the world.

The Middle East does not need bloody revolutions or new tyrannies, but it does desperately need change. It is the oldest civilized area on Earth and in the past its people were masters of art, science, and commerce, but in the present it is a wilderness of wasted human potential. This is not solely the fault of the United States, but its presence and its policies have certainly reinforced the status quo. Now, the United States is probably going home, so we shall all soon find out if leaving the Middle East to its own devices brings on the disasters that some of the pillars of the present order, American, Arab, and Israeli alike, continually predict. We will also find out what is left of America's position in the world.

The United States has lost its way before, plumbing the depths of defeat and global opprobrium during the Vietnam War, and it bounced back virtually unscathed in terms of its ability to influence events in the world. Big and terrible though it was, the conflict in Vietnam, even in America's own eyes, was only a border skirmish in a much larger and longer confrontation, the Cold War. Disagreements between the United States and its many allies were mainly about such tactical questions as whether Vietnam was the right place to fight, not about such fundamental issues as whether the United States should be the leader of the "Free World" or who the enemy was. This time is different.

Early in 2002, partly in response to the shock of 9/11 but also as an expression of the hubris that had swept American political circles since the end of the Cold War, the United States did something that it had not done even in the depths of the Cold War, when John F. Kennedy was promising to "pay any price and bear any burden" in order to contain Soviet "expansionism": it officially laid claim to a status above that of other countries and also above international law. "I will not wait on events while dangers gather," said President Bush in his "axis of evil" State of the Union message on January 29, 2002. "I will not stand by as peril draws closer and closer. The United States will not permit the world's most dangerous regimes to threaten us with the world's most destructive weapons." It was, as strategic analyst Ivo Daalder said at the time, "a virtual declaration of war. It enunciated a new doctrine, which says that people we declare bad, with weapons we declare bad, are basically the same as terrorists." So Bush invaded Iraq.

Three years later, with the Iraq adventure falling apart, Bush was still making the same claim of a special status for America that allows it to act militarily without the support of other countries or of the United Nations. His "National Security Strategy" report to Congress in March 2006 again made the assertion that the United States would attack any country that it felt was dangerous, in complete disregard of international law: "If necessary . . . we do not rule out the use of force before attacks occur – even if uncertainty remains as to the time and place of the enemy's attack. . . . The place of pre-emption in our national security strategy remains the same." Then he speculated publicly about attacking Iran. It could still have been 2002, when politicos and pundits in Washington confidently spoke about remaking the world in the image of the United States.

The regimes that richly deserve to be overthrown and replaced are not confined to the three singled-out members of the axis of evil. At a minimum, the axis should extend to Syria and Lebanon and Libya, as well as "friends" of America like the Saudi royal family and Egypt's Hosni Mubarak, along with the Palestinian Authority, whether headed by Arafat or one of his henchmen.

There is no denying that the alternative to these regimes could easily turn out to be worse, even (or especially) if it comes into power through democratic elections. After all . . . very large numbers of people in the Muslim world sympathize with Osama bin Laden and would vote for radical Islamic candidates of his stripe if they were given the chance.

... Nevertheless, there is a policy that can head it off, provided that the United States has the will to fight World War IV – the war against militant Islam – to a successful conclusion, and provided, too, that we then have the stomach to impose a new political culture on the defeated parties.

– Norman Podhoretz, "In Praise of the Bush Doctrine," *Commentary*, September 2002

Norman Podhoretz is in many ways the intellectual godfather of the neo-conservatives. He wrote those half-crazed lines, which envisaged the United States attacking Iraq, Iran, North Korea, Syria, Lebanon, Libya, Saudi Arabia, Egypt, and the Palestinian occupied territories and holding them all down with U.S. troops long enough for Americans to "impose a new political culture on the defeated parties," at a time when American power was as hugely overestimated in other countries as it was in Washington itself. Many people were genuinely afraid that the United States could and would do such things. But it is no longer 2002, and neither the Iranians nor anybody else thinks that the United States can run the world. Now the United States is widely seen, as one senior Japanese foreign ministry official told me last year, as "a twelve-year-old with a shotgun": dangerous, but not serious.

The United States is a great deal more than that, but the country's reputation has taken a terrible battering in the past few years. In an opinion poll taken in November 2006 in the four countries traditionally closest to the United States in their international views, Canada, Mexico, Britain, and Israel, President Bush was seen as a danger to world peace by more respondents (75 per cent) than North Korean dictator Kim Jong-Il (69 per cent), Iranian president Mahmoud Ahmadinejad (62 per cent), and Hassan Nasrallah, the leader of Hezbollah (62 per cent). In the United States it is traditional to dismiss such views as "anti-American," as though negative judgments of American foreign policy are necessarily irrational, but even if you assume that all those foreigners are driven by blind prejudice, the numbers have never looked like this before. And world public opinion matters, even for the United States.

In the Vietnam era, the last time that there were grave and widespread doubts in every part of the world about American foreign policy, the United States still accounted for about 40 per cent of the industrial capacity of the entire planet, and its role as the "leader of the Free World" was unquestioned. Critics were concerned that America was leading everybody in the wrong direction, not that it was the wrong leader. But things are very different now. The U.S. economy accounts for only about 20 per cent of world economic activity, and its share of manufacturing is much lower than that. There is no international consensus that "terrorism" or "militant Islam" is the world's greatest threat, or that everybody else must follow the United States in a generation-long crusade against it. On the contrary, in many parts of the world there are grave doubts about the direction of American policy, and some suspicions, too.

The more generous senior officials in the countries that are America's traditional friends and allies tend to assume that the Americans have just gone off their heads for a while, and will recover their balance sooner or later (though not under the current administration). The more suspicious ones wonder if this is not a U.S. attempt to reassert global leadership and control by generating a consciously exaggerated scare. By the time you get to less friendly capitals like Moscow and Beijing, that is probably the majority position. Either way, it isn't going to work. The United States will not be given carte blanche by other countries to take charge in this "emergency." On the contrary, most countries are waiting for the American adventure in Iraq to fail with a keen sense of curiosity about what that will do to the global pecking order.

International power does not depend solely on resources, money, and weapons, though you cannot have it without those things. It depends also on reputation: a reputation for honest dealing, for consistency, for success. No country, not even the United States at the moment of its greatest triumph, the victory in the Second World War, is so powerful that it can neglect these factors – but it had them then, in spades. In the late 1940s, and all the way through the 1950s, America was seen by most of the non-Communist world as the shining City on the Hill. American diplomats were deferred to, American intentions were rarely questioned, and American competence was assumed.

That uncritical admiration came to an end with the Vietnam War: the United States was revealed as a country like the others, capable of committing huge errors and great cruelties. But the wounds that the Vietnam War inflicted on the United States' reputation were much shallower than they appeared, and healed quickly. By the late 1980s and early 1990s, the United States was seen once again as an extremely useful international citizen and a natural leader, albeit without the starry-eyed admiration of earlier years. But the current U.S. adventures in the Middle East are having a more profoundly damaging effect on America's reputation, because they call into question its motives and even its basic competence. This is occurring at a time, moreover, when its relative power in the world is already on the slide, due to the emergence of new great powers in Asia. The Iraq fiasco has created the potential for a big drop in the United States' influence in the world: invading a country with one-twelfth of its population illegally, without provocation, and on false pretexts, and then mismanaging the occupation so badly that it loses the subsequent guerrilla war, suggests that the United States is not only a dangerously erratic superpower but a seriously incompetent one. If it follows up by attacking Iran, the loss of power will be precipitous and largely irreversible. As Zbigniew Brzezinski put it, the United States will "lose its place in the world."

This is not a desirable outcome: the twentieth century would have ended much less happily if not for the enormous and mostly benign influence of the United States. But it is increasingly becoming a likely outcome.